Ethics in AMERICA

DANTES/DSST* Study Guide

All rights reserved. This Study Guide, Book and Flashcards are protected under the US Copyright Law. No part of this book or study guide or flashcards may be reproduced, distributed or stored in a retrieval system, or transmitted in any form or by any means, electronic, mechanical, photocopying, recording, or otherwise, without the prior written permission of the publisher Breely Crush Publishing, LLC.

© 2015 Breely Crush Publishing, LLC

*DSST is a registered trademark of The Thomson Corporation and its affiliated companies, and does not endorse this book.

971060415143

Copyright ©2003 - 2015, Breely Crush Publishing, LLC.

All rights reserved.

This Study Guide, Book and Flashcards are protected under the US Copyright Law. No part of this publication may be reproduced, distributed or stored in a retrieval system, or transmitted in any form or by any means, electronic, mechanical, photocopying, recording, or otherwise, without the prior written permission of the publisher Breely Crush Publishing, LLC.

Published by Breely Crush Publishing, LLC
10808 River Front Parkway
South Jordan, UT 84095
www.breelycrushpublishing.com

ISBN-10: 1-61433-046-8
ISBN-13: 978-1-61433-046-2

Printed and bound in the United States of America.

DSST is a registered trademark of The Thomson Corporation and its affiliated companies, and does not endorse this book.

Table of Contents

Section 1 – Ethical Traditions 1
Greek View: Thucydides, Socrates, Plato, Aristotle 1
Relationship of Morality to the Community 1
Duty to Obey the Law 2
Relationship Between Self-Interest and Virtue 3
Relationship Between Virtue and Happiness 4
Concepts of Justice 5
Justice as the Interest of the Stronger 5
Justice as Playing the Proper Role 6
Equity as Proper Ratio of Benefits 7
Virtue and Human Natures 7
Nature and Kings of Virtue 8
Virtue as Excellence 9
Virtue, Habit and Character 9
Voluntary Action 10
Doctrine of the Mean 11
The Best Human Life 11
Biblical Traditions: Books of the Law, Prophets, Gospels and Writings of Paul .. 12
Relationship Between Law and Morality 14
Role of the Covenant 14
Role of the Prophets in Denouncing Evil 15
Conceptions of Justice in Punishment and in the Distribution of Wealth ... 15
Relationship Between Morality and Community 16
Place of Mercy and Love 16
Apparent Paradoxes in the Traditions 16
Moral Law: Epictetus, Aquinas, Hobbes, Locke, Jefferson, Kant, etc. 17
View of Human Nature 18
Basis of Natural Law 18
Principle of Double Effect 19
Metaethics 19
Natural Rights and Duties 20
Relationship of Natural Law to Religious Belief 20
Source of Political Authority 21
Social Contract 21
Relationship of Natural Law and Human Law 22
Just War Theory 22
Justifiability of Revolution or Civil Disobedience 23
Equality and Liberty 23
Deontological vs. Consequential Moral Frameworks 24

Hypothetical and Categorical Imperatives 24
Good Will and Duty for its Own Sake 25
Persons as Ends in Themselves Not as Means Only 25
Loyalty and Virtue 25
Vices 26
Relationship of Morality to Self-Interest and Happiness 27
Conceptions of Justice 27
Fairness and Distributive Justice 28
Euthanasia 28
Consequential Ethics: Epicurus, Bentham, Mill 29
Consequential vs. Deontological Moral Frameworks 29
Hedonism and Kinds of Pleasure 30
Self-Interest or Prudence and the Common Good 30
Joel Feinberg 31
Friedrich Nietzsche 31
Principle of Utility or Greatest Happiness Principle 32
Felicific Calculus 32
Conscience and External Sanctions of Morality 32
Self-Regarding and Other Regarding Conduct 33
Individual Liberty and the Limits of the State's Authority 33
Feminist Ethics 34
Ayn Rand 35
Jane English 35
Religious Belief Systems 35
Primal Religions 36
Native North American Traditions 37
Social Dharma 38
David Gauthier 39
Critique of Standard Ethics 39
Alternative Visions – Care Ethic and Ethic of Trust 40
Medical Ethics 40
Sample Test Questions Section 1: Ethical Traditions 41
Doing Good, Not Doing Harm, Preventing Harm 48
Obligations to Strangers 49
Special Moral Relationships 50
Conflict of Duties 51
Autonomy and Privacy 51
Fidelity, Accountability and Trustworthiness 52
Veracity 53
Right to Information 53
Confidentiality 54

Informed Consent...54
Institutional Responsibilities..56
Professional Code of Ethics...56
Paternalism..56
Retributive and Distributive Justice 57
Ronald Dworkin..58
Balancing Harms..58
Ethics and Environmental Ties 59
Environmental Racism..59
Sample Test Questions Section 2: Ethical Analysis 60
Answers to Sample Test Questions (32-100)...69
Additional Sample Test Questions 72
Test-Taking Strategies 98
Test Preparation...99
Legal Note...99

Section 1 – Ethical Traditions

The subject of ethics has been argued for centuries. Ethics is the often considered to be the science of human duty or how to determine the rules for right and wrong. Throughout history, there have been many traditions or schools of thought, concerning what it means to be ethical. Some of the more popular traditions have included the Greek and the Biblical traditions but there has also developed more modern traditions as well.

In this course we will examine some of the more popular proponents of ethical tradition and some of the ideas that they have presented. Having studied those different traditions and ideas, we will then examine the differences between them and you can decide for yourself which theories you feel are most valuable.

Greek View: Thucydides, Socrates, Plato, Aristotle

The Early Greek view is one of the most widely studied ethical traditions in all of philosophy. The most influential mind to ever emerge from this tradition is Socrates. However, Socrates would never have been known by modern day scholars if it were not for his closest student Plato. Plato is also considered to be one of the most popular Greek philosophers of all time. Plato wrote down Socrates ideas and later started a school in Athens called the "Academy of Plato." Aristotle was also a very great philosopher at this time that studied at Plato's school and later opened his own school in Athens called the "Peripatetic School." These three great philosophers, Socrates, Plato and Aristotle are thought to be the "giants" of Greek philosophy. Still, there are many other famous Greeks such as Thucydides and Plotinus who contributed to Greek thought in many significant ways.

Relationship of Morality to the Community

One of the major debates in the Greek tradition involves the relationship between morality and the community. What is the duty that a person has to their community?

Socrates opinion is best understood through example he made of his life. He was never politically active but he did fight courageously in two different battles when he was still fairly young. He also never argued for or against the ruling political system of his time but he was later held suspect by members of the regime and was killed for a charge that is still debated in classrooms today.

Because of the general nervous atmosphere in Athens during the time, Socrates was accused of "corrupting the youth." There had been many attacks on the traditional beliefs of the government at that time and many officials believed that Socrates was a threat to the democratic government. They had him arrested and sentenced him to death.

Socrates said that he had never intended to corrupt the Athenian youth but had only meant to inspire them to think for themselves. In this way, he believed that people could fulfill their duty to their community as ethical individuals. His method of philosophical inquiry is known as the "Socratic Method" and is a way of argument in which a person seeks to discover the truth about a certain issue.

After Socrates was sentenced to death, Plato carried on his ideas and wrote a very famous book entitled Plato's Republic. In this book, Plato explains the duties that an ethical person should have to their community. He describes a form of government known as the Republic that is lead by a Philosopher King.

The Republic has many officials in it who work at various levels. The Philosopher King is said to be an appropriate leader because he has had a profound vision about the reality of the world which helps him to guide others in the community. This vision that comes to the Philosopher King is described in one of the most famous passages of Plato's Republic known as the "Allegory of the Cave."

Duty to Obey the Law

Socrates was a law abiding citizen and believed that the duty of obeying the law came from the gratitude that a person should have for its benefits. Without laws, many negative things would have likely befallen a person and so it is important to have a respect for the law and to obey it to the best of your ability.

Of course, problems can often arise between what is "right" and what is "legal." Sometimes there are extenuating circumstances where ethical decisions involve a conflict with the law. This problem was taken up by Aristotle in his famous work entitled Nicomachean Ethics.

For Aristotle, justice was the most important virtue a person could have. His idea of justice included the common adhering to the law but also included "natural justice" which could sometimes cause confusion between what was ethically right and what was legal. For Aristotle, there was such a concept as "equity" which was applicable in certain cases when an ethical act was corrective of the law and therefore stood above it. Aristotle said that some laws could become obsolete to the point of being absurd. In this case, the law would need to be changed. However, Aristotle warned about wanting to change the laws too often and stressed that most instances of the law should be justly followed.

Thucydides was another Greek philosopher who was the author of The Peloponnesian War. He also taught about the importance of adhering to the law but was a strong proponent of free speech. He believed in allowing an ease in private relations between citizens but did not condone lawlessness. He taught that the magistrates and the laws of the time should be obeyed, particularly in regard to protecting the injured.

Thrasymachus was a philosopher who lived around 500 BC. He believed that justice was the struggle between different powers trying to gain advantage over one another. He believed that "might makes right." Thucydides lived around the same time. He believed that "Right, as the world goes, is only in question between equals in power, while the strong do what they can and the weak suffer what they must." Although his belief is similar to Thrasymachus's, there are distinctions. Thucydides felt that power struggle could also be harmful to democracy. This is the main different between the two because although Thucydides had a similar belief about the essential meaning of justice, he believed that it had a negative side. Also, Thrasymachus's view of justice requires there to be powers in struggle, whereas Thucydides's view believes power struggle a danger to justice.

Relationship Between Self-Interest and Virtue

The Greek philosophers often discussed the connection between one's own self-interest and the higher quality of being virtuous. They never seemed to be capable of envisioning a virtue that was completely devoid of any self-interest. This may not have been the case for Socrates, who sacrificed his life for his beliefs. Still, for Plato and Aristotle, it seemed to be an irreconcilable problem.

Plato thought it was impossible to be virtuous without at least thinking of yourself a little bit. He believed that a person always did the thing that they thought was best but often made mistakes about it and had to learn the hard way. He saw people as basically innocent but his ideal state of virtue was never completely devoid of at least some self-interest. This idea is very characteristic of Greek ethics. They often refused to consider the possibility of a conflict between self-interest and virtue.

This conflict, however, is also debated in relation to Aristotle's philosophy. In order to overcome what was suggested as a conflict, Aristotle tried to show that acting to benefit others contributed to one's own happiness and therefore was in one's own self-interest. There was nothing wrong with self-interest and there was no conflict. His argument ran into problems however as he would later assert that a truly virtuous person would only practice altruism for its own sake. With altruism containing even the slightest bit of self-interest, others would eventually say it was selfish and the argument would become like an endless circle.

Regardless of the difficulties in dealing with the reality of self-interest, the ethics of Aristotle and Plato placed the main emphasis on virtue. They recognized the reality of self-interest but still held firmly to virtue as the main ideal for a moral life. Socrates chose death to teach a greater moral lesson to the people of Athens and, for this reason; he has been considered the most influential of the Greek philosophers.

Relationship Between Virtue and Happiness

Although Socrates died for his beliefs about what was right and wrong, there was one Greek philosopher who believed that a person could be both completely virtuous and happy without having to sacrifice their body. This was the famous Greek philosopher known as Plotinus.

Plotinus was the founder of Neo-Platonism or "The New-Platonism" which was sort of like a scientific philosophy of religion. Neo-Platonism taught that the "One" or "The Good" was the source of all things. Plotinus wanted to build a city called Platonopolis which was to be governed according to the model discussed in Plato's Republic. Still, his dream was never realized. Plotinus' famous work is entitled The Enneads and it discusses the nature of the Soul and the relation of the Soul to Divine Unity.

Plato had taught that "The Good" transcended both "Being" and the "World of Forms and Ideas." Plotinus simply took those teachings and used them to develop his own philosophy about virtue and happiness. Plotinus also got some of his ideas from Aristotle who taught that there was a "First Cause" that was transcendent and the ultimate source of the intellect. By using both Plato and Aristotle's ideas, Plotinus then went on to teach that the body could be illuminated by the Soul and this could lead a person to happiness.

Plotinus developed a system which combined many ideas from classical Greek philosophy. By combining these ideas he developed the idea of a "First Principle" of reality. This First Principle was also referred to as a "Oneness" or "Unity" which incorporated virtue in such a way as to help a person's Soul transcend all Being and bring happiness.

Concepts of Justice

Although Plotinus' dream of building a city called Platonopolis was never realized, it is interesting to imagine what this city would have been like. For Plato, the concept of Justice was a very central issue in his philosophy and one that Plotinus would have likely had to put to use in a city like Platonopolis.

In fact, Plato discussed two main principles of political justice that he though were most fundamental to a proposal for government. The first principle was that of securing the potential for each member of society to experience "The Good." Each person would likely have a different way of reaching The Good and these would have to be secured. A society could only be just if each member was allowed to play their own social class role which was defined by the persons "nature."

The second principle of Plato's theory of justice had to do with maximizing the results of each person's efforts through applying their "natures" fairly in the society. The inequalities of people would have to be arranged so that certain benefits were awarded and fairly satisfied the "natural desires" of each person.

For Plato, there was an intimate connection between a person's nature and their path to The Good. Each person's nature was made up of the things that they desired most and this expressed what the pathway to The Good would be for them. This connection between a person's nature and The Good was crucial to the understanding of Platonic political justice.

Socrates had given these ideas to Plato and told him that "everyone must practice one of the occupations in the city for which he is naturally best suited." Socrates also foresaw the problem that people might have with the special benefits that some members might receive over others. Nevertheless, he saw this unequal treatment of certain officials in society as being a necessary requirement in establishing order in that society.

 ## Justice as the Interest of the Stronger

Socrates had often argued about the different conceptions of justice but never really came to a concrete definition that had satisfied him. This was a common problem among the Greeks and one that especially aggravated Thrasymachus.

In a very famous debate, Thrasymachus makes a very violent and impatient remark to Socrates and yells out "Stop talking nonsense and look into the facts! Justice is nothing else than the interest of the stronger!" Thrasymachus' impatience with Socrates had led him to believe the worst. There was no such thing as justice and it was only the dominant political or social group of any city that instituted laws and governed for its own benefit.

This challenge by Thrasymachus has been a point of debate among philosophers for centuries. In fact, two philosophical positions still exist today that are based in this very kind of thinking; Moral Skepticism and Relativism.

After presenting his statement, Thrasymachus first intends to leave the dialogue as if to say that his statement is so true that no further debate about justice would ever be necessary. Still, Socrates was not convinced by his statement and went on to argue with him in a calm and deliberate tone. "Should we really believe that justice is really the good of another, the advantage of the stronger and the ruler, harmful to the one who obeys, while injustice is in one's own advantage?"

In this famous dialogue, Socrates finally succeeds in showing Thrasymachus that his position is self-contradictory. Thrasymachus does indeed withdraw from the dialogue but with a red face. He was still, however, not completely convinced. In fact, there are many people today who are not convinced by Socrates dialogues and Thrasymachus statement still lingers even today.

Justice as Playing the Proper Role

In the same way that self-interest and virtue tended to take on a circular form of reasoning in Aristotle's philosophy, justice and the proper role of distributing rewards tends to take on a circular argument with him as well.

Aristotle's idea of justice is defined in terms of situational factors that exist outside of the "just" person. Situations and communities are only just when the people receive their proper benefits according to what they deserve. Although he was very extensive about trying to define his terms and used a famous doctrine known as the "Doctrine of the Mean," there was still a problem which ultimately arose for Aristotle. The things that people deserved were always largely defined by how "just" they were in the first place. This made for an endless circle that many people still argue over today.

Both Plato and Aristotle were rationalists and they both emphasized the role of reason in perceiving what is just. They discouraged the act of giving in to contrary impulses or desires when trying to determine what is right or wrong. Thrasymachus gave into anger in his argument with Socrates and this was certainly not held to be a virtue. Nonetheless, something was missing in the Greeks reasoning that might only have been satisfied by subsequent philosophers of later generations.

Plotinus chose to rise above the arguments and to put concepts like justice in their proper place as activities rather than as concrete thoughts or objects. He said that "Justice is not the thought of Justice but an activity of the Intellectual Principle and an appearance so lovely that neither evening nor dawn is so fair."

Equity as Proper Ratio of Benefits

As we have discussed earlier, there are sometimes conflicts which can arise between what is "right" and what is "legal." For Aristotle, the idea of justice includes the common idea of adhering to the law but it also includes the idea of "natural justice."

Natural justice is something that is always the same in any time or place. It is determined by the laws of the universe and may be difficult to see in many cases. This is because of the fact that governments often differ in their definitions of right and wrong and there is no perfect legal system. However, Aristotle thought that any legal justice needed to do its best to be in accordance with natural justice.

In order to stay in accordance with natural justice, Aristotle used the concept of "equity" as the solution to any disparity between natural justice and legal justice. When an ethical act was needed to correct the law, an appeal to equity could be made and could expose an extraordinary case in which more fairness was needed. This would appeal to what Aristotle called "the sort of justice which goes beyond written law" and could be used in any case.

An example of a case involving equity as proper ratio of benefits might be a case in a divorce court where a wife was asking for extra money from her husband after a divorce that had special circumstances. If the wife had supported her husband all through college by working as a waitress, she might be entitled to an extra ratio of alimony based on the fact that she had sacrificed her own education to support her husband. Due to an appeal for equity, the proper distribution of benefits to the wife would be higher than a typical divorce might require.

Virtue and Human Natures

Socrates would often question the idea of virtue with the other Greek philosophers and show them how their ideas about virtue were never complete. Having learned from Socrates, Plato tried to develop a reasonable set of answers about what it meant to be virtuous and to pass these ideas on to Aristotle at his Academy.

Still, Aristotle never felt satisfied with Plato's ideas either. He developed his own ideas about virtue that were also argued over throughout Greek history. The quest for an understanding about virtue was an ongoing subject amongst the Greeks that ended with Plotinus development of Neo-Platonism.

Plotinus had taken the ideas from Plato about the World of Forms and had developed these ideas to explain how a person could overcome their human nature and reach The Good. The World of Forms was something that had to be observed by the Soul and then transcended. Forms are sort of like qualities that all objects in the world participate in. There is the Form of "Beauty" and the Form of "Largeness" or "Smallness." Plato believed that we could never intelligently say that some particular object was beautiful unless we had a prior acquaintance with "Beauty" itself.

For Plato, there were an infinite number of Forms. If a person observed the way they thought about things and the way they experienced things, they would see their own mental creation of "Forms" projected on to the world and eventually transcend their own human nature. This experience was also described in "The Allegory of the Cave."

Plotinus thought that observing one's own nature, a person's Soul could transcend the World of Forms and become truly virtuous so that they could eventually achieve union with the One. This was similar to what Socrates had described in The Allegory of the Cave. The person would have to first observe their own human nature and transcend their physical body by pursuing an ascetic lifestyle. This meant turning away from the material world and looking inward to the Soul.

Plotinus was intensely aware of how reason and human rationality, especially as it was expressed in language, was limited. He thought that it could never bring the kind of answers that the Greeks were searching for. Instead, he proposed a more observational approach into one's own human nature. By looking at ones human nature and their relationship to the universe, a person could become unified with the One.

 Nature and Kings of Virtue

As previously discussed, Plato taught his students about virtue and about the idea of the "Philosopher-King" who had obtained a vision so great that he was capable of properly leading people in a good society. If you remember, the vision that comes to the Philosopher-King is explained in Plato's famous book The Republic in a famous story known as "the Allegory of the Cave."

In the Allegory of the Cave, Plato recalls a story by Socrates where a man is chained to the wall inside a cave. The story is meant to symbolize the natural state of man's existence. Socrates explains that nature dictates how men view the world. It is just as if they had been chained their whole lives to the wall of a cave. Because of nature, men have never really seen the outside world that exists beyond the cave. In Socrates story, the cave is described as very dark and men can only see shadows that flash across the wall. They can only dream of being free and experiencing the truth that lies behind these shadows.

The Philosopher-King, however, is an exceptionally virtuous man who has learned how to break his chains and walk outside the cave. The Philosopher-King has looked upon the real world and, after adjusting his eyes to the light of the Sun, is capable of returning to the cave and teaching others how to break their chains and live a virtuous life. These "Kings of Virtue" are the few men and women who truly understand what it means to be virtuous and to live a free life.

Virtue as Excellence

After hearing about the vision of the Cave, we may ask ourselves "How are we to follow the teachings of Socrates and Plato and become virtuous? How do we see outside the Cave?" Since Aristotle was one of the greatest students of these two philosophers, it would help us to look at what he has said in terms of virtue and excellence.

Aristotle explained that virtue was a manner of behaving that brought a full experience of happiness in a person's life. He wasn't talking about a happiness that lasted a few hours or even a few days. Aristotle was talking about behaving in such a way that you achieved an ongoing sense of happiness in your life which he called "Eudaimonia."

This happiness that Aristotle talked about came from having an excellently active lifestyle. He said that human virtue was like having a kind of excellence in your life and that this excellence came from always using your reasoning to guide your actions. For Aristotle, being virtuous meant being very good at something or to excel in something. For Aristotle, that excellence was determined through a person's own reasoning skills. The main thing about being virtuous, however, was learning how to be happy or achieving "Eudaimonia" in your life.

Virtue, Habit and Character

Aristotle always gave sound advice on how to become virtuous. His ideas were always simple and full of common sense. He insisted that excellence always came from developing good habits which would eventually lead to good character.

How does a person develop good habits? Of course it takes a lot of consistent effort over a certain number of days to develop a habit in our lives. At first we have a little trouble sticking to our plan but when we keep at it for a certain amount of time, it eventually turns into a habit and we don't even notice we are doing it anymore. This is just one example of how we use our reasoning to build our character and become more virtuous.

Of course everyone is born with different skills and talents. Some people are good at math while others are good at sports. By using our reasoning, however, we can determine which things we are better at and then make a little effort to improve the things that we aren't very good at. By creating better habits in the areas that we tend to have weaknesses, we can eventually build a strong character and achieve virtue.

This form of reasoning that Aristotle suggested was based on a theory called the "Doctrine of the Mean." This doctrine generally explained that it is important never to do too much of any one thing. Rather, it is best to try and improve in the areas that you are a little bit weak. In this way, you can bring those areas that you are weak a little bit closer to the areas where you are strong. Eventually you can achieve a strong character and bring about a virtue that leads to Eudaimonia or happiness in your life.

Voluntary Action

Aristotle also felt that voluntary action was an important part of the formula for achieving virtue and happiness in life. If you are going to use your reasoning to learn to create better habits in your life, Aristotle thought that it was extremely important that you do these things through your own voluntary action.

He didn't think it was possible for a person to gain any virtue whatsoever if they created their habits only because somebody else made them do it. Actions that are produced by somebody else, perhaps under extreme duress are done so involuntarily. The person who is learning to do them is not responsible for them and therefore does not acquire any real virtue from these habits.

If someone were to grab your arm and use it to hit someone, would you be responsible for that!? Aristotle thought that a person could not reasonably be blamed or praised for something that they had done mostly as a result of what others made them do. Actions performed out of ignorance were also considered to be involuntary according to Aristotle. Thus, if you were swinging your arm for exercise and you hit someone by accident, then you couldn't be held responsible for that either. Of course, this was no excuse for neglecting your own responsibilities and it was also important that a person exercised their own awareness at all times so as to avoid accidents whenever possible.

Aristotle thought that a voluntary action relied on deliberation about the choice that a person was making. This meant that the person had to be aware of all the options that were available and then, after evaluating them all in light of the good, they chose the best option among all of them. Only in this way could people properly develop their character and eventually obtain Eudaimonia in their lives.

Doctrine of the Mean

The Doctrine of the Mean was developed by Aristotle as a method for determining what the virtuous thing to do in a situation. For Aristotle, there were two types of mean that needed to be considered. The first mean was called the absolute mean and it was the thing that was considered equidistant or right in the middle of the two absolute extremes of a given behavior or amount. For example, the absolute mean of a steak dinner would be halfway between all the steak in the world and no steak whatsoever. Aristotle thought that this mean was not really so important and wouldn't really help us to decide on our behavior. The relative mean, however, was much more important and needed to be determined for all virtuous actions.

The relative mean represented that which was neither "too much" nor "too little" for any given person. Of course, this relative mean was not the same for everyone. Instead, it was something that had to be determined more as an art form than a mathematical calculation and it told us how much was right for us.

According to Aristotle then, we may say that a virtuous person always avoids what is too much and what is too little. He or she will seek for the mean and choose it. It wouldn't be the absolute mean but rather the relative mean that would determine how much was right for us. In this way, virtue was considered to be a kind of self-moderation.

The Best Human Life

One of Socrates most famous sayings is that "an unexamined life is not worth living." Apart from all the arguments and theories that all the Greek philosophers had, Socrates always emerged from them as the supreme questioner. He never stopped asking questions even when there had been so many answers that had been given to him all along the way.

It was Socrates belief that people became better simply by asking the questions that came to their minds and, if they were forbidden from doing this, their life would not be worth living. He was never satisfied with the easy and quick answers to things. He always chose to look deeper and to raise more questions in a quest for the Truth. In this way, people were moved to greatness by Socrates teachings and they would go on to achieve better things with their lives for many years to come.

Although many other Greeks like Thrasymachus and the officials of Athens often became frustrated with Socrates methods, he never backed down. He was eventually threatened with death but insisted that asking questions was the best way to live a human life. He felt so strongly about this that he even faced death in order to uphold his beliefs. Today, Socrates is considered the giant of the Greek philosophers and his "Socratic Method" for questioning things still remains a respected ideal for students everywhere.

Biblical Traditions: Books of the Law, Prophets, Gospels and Writings of Paul

Jesus said that "All the Law and the Prophets hang upon the Two Great Commandments, to love thy Lord God and to love thy neighbor." These books that he was referring to are the Books of the Law and the Prophets and they make up the entire Old Testament of the Bible. The first five books of the Old Testament are called the Books of the Law because they are considered to contain the laws and instruction given to the people of Israel. These books, Genesis to Deuteronomy, lay the foundation for the coming of Christ. The Book of the Prophets is the second section of the Old Testament and is also the largest section of the entire Bible. Some of the books of the Prophets are Isaiah, Jeremiah, Ezekiel, Joshua, Judges, Samuel and Kings.

The New Testament has 27 books that also fall into two sections. The first section is the Gospels which tell the story of Jesus. They are the books of Matthew, Mark, Luke and John. The second section is the Letters. The Letters were mostly written by Paul and provide guidance for the earliest church communities.

Cain and Abel

In the Bible, Cain and Abel were the children of Adam and Eve. Both Cain and Abel were supposed to make sacrifices to the Lord. As was commanded, Abel offered an animal sacrifice. Cain, on the other hand, offered the "fruit of the ground" as his sacrifice, and it was not accepted by the Lord. Cain killed his brother Abel out of greed and jealousy, hoping to advance his position. However, the Lord knew of Cain's treachery, and he was punished. Cain did not follow the commandments of the Lord, and was not able to hide his sin. For this reason, Cain is considered the first murderer and Abel the first martyr.

Amos

Amos was a farmer who lived in the kingdom of Judah, but was called by the Lord to preach in Israel. The people were hardening their hearts against the Lord, and Amos called them to repentance from their many sins. The wealthy were becoming increasingly wealthy at the expense of the poor. Amos proclaimed that all people are on the same level in God's eyes, and He expects the same purity of them all. Meaning that all people are essentially the same, and wealth, position, and birthright don't change the application of ethics.

Exodus

In the Book of Exodus, Moses is called to lead the people out of bondage in Egypt and into the Promised Land. Of course, the Pharaoh does not want the people to leave. Moses then has to use the plagues to convince him. Once the people are out of Egypt, the Lord makes a covenant with the Israelites and they agree to be his people. It is at this time that the Ten Commandments and the Law of Moses are set forth. These laws provide a moral base for the people to live off of, discussing rules relating from cleanliness to politics to religion.

Much of the Old Testament of the Bible is associated with the Law of Moses. Detailed and ritualistic, the Law of Moses includes the Ten Commandments, and detailed laws concerning morality, business dealing, politics, worship, and physical purity. It discussed everything from personal cleanliness to priestly duties, essentially eliminating the need for a person to exercise conscience.

The Law of Retaliation comes from the Law of Moses in the Oldest Testament of the Bible. The essence of it is "an eye for an eye." Or in other words, the punishment is equal to the wrongdoing. The main ethical application of the Law of Retaliation is the struggle between justice and mercy. The Law of Retaliation is completely just, but allows no place for mercy.

Sermon on the Mount

The Sermon on the Mount was a sermon given by Jesus, the account of which is in Matthew chapters 5-7. In a way, the Sermon on the Mount is Jesus's commentary on the Ten Commandments. Because of this, the Sermon on the Mount could be considered a summary of Christian ethical beliefs. Its topics include attitude, murder, adultery, marriage, oaths, forgiveness, prayer, false prophets, and judgment.

Relationship Between Law and Morality

In the early books of the Bible, we first learn about two main characters; Abraham and Jacob. Abraham is the person through whom God establishes his covenant with the people of Israel. Later we learn about Jacob who is a descendant of Abraham. Jacob's family has many problems and Jacob himself did not really have a strong system of ethics. Instead of having a system of his own, he simply equated morality with legality. Whatever was within the law was morally right for Jacob. For this reason, he was somewhat of a manipulator when it came to getting what he wanted. With this kind of mentality Jacob was not much different from a lot of the Jews of Jesus' time. The Jews felt that being a descendant of Abraham assured them of God's favor and they were confident that by simply sticking to the law of the land that they would be acceptable to God.

In the Bible, Jesus comes along and shows the Jews that a much greater form of ethics is necessary if you want to go to Heaven. For Jesus, the law is only a minimum standard. It is important to follow the law but it is even more important to have a genuine faith in God. These two requirements were not in conflict with each other but were to both be followed if a person was going to eventually get to Heaven.

Role of the Covenant

One of the reasons that the Jews of Jesus' time were so confident about their favor with God was that they had been taught about a covenant that had been made many years before. Their ancestor Abraham had been told by God "In thee and thy seed shall all the nations of the earth be blessed." Abraham had been told by God that his grandchildren would be chosen to fulfill a Divine plan for the salvation of God's children.

The Old Testament tells the story of these people who, because God chose Abraham and his grandchildren as the hosts of this great event, thought that they were all assured of going to Heaven. This was not entirely true in the manner that they thought, however. The people of Israel were indeed chosen to introduce Jesus their Savior to humanity but this didn't mean that they could simply do as they pleased. The covenant was simply a promise that told of the coming of a Savior and told that the people of Israel would introduce this Savior to the world. They would certainly be lucky to have been chosen but their own salvation would be much more complex. The Old Testament is full of stories which anticipate the coming of Jesus with great excitement.

Role of the Prophets in Denouncing Evil

The Old Testament is filled with many strong objections to evil or unethical behavior. This was not the main focus of Jesus teachings in the New Testament as he said "All the Law and the Prophets hang upon the Two Great Commandments, to love thy Lord God and to love thy neighbor." Although Jesus certainly did not engage in any activity that might be considered "evil", it was not an important focus of his teachings to denounce evil as it was for the earlier teachings in the prophets.

Because of this distinction between how the prophets taught the people and how Jesus taught the people, the books of the Bible are divided into the Old and New Testaments. One exception to this rule, however, is the book of revelations which is contained at the end of the New Testament. This book also contains strong language denouncing evil in its many forms and was written by an author whose associations with Jesus are not completely known.

With the passing of the role of the prophets in denouncing evil, we have what is considered to be a new law under Jesus which stresses the importance of faith and love rather than condemnation.

Conceptions of Justice in Punishment and in the Distribution of Wealth

In terms of punishment, Jesus was not an advocate of this. Rather, his teachings focused on practicing forgiveness of others and his most significant example of this came when his enemies killed him on the cross. As he was being crucified, Jesus said "Forgive them Father, for they know not what they do."

In terms of the distribution of wealth, Jesus responded to a question about paying taxes to the emperor. He said, "Give unto Caesar what is Caesars, give unto God what is Gods." This teaching follows a similar idea as what has been discussed previously in terms of legality and morality in the Bible. What is legal is not always entirely moral but the two do not have to be in conflict. A person should pay their taxes and follow the law but they should also be concerned with their Faith and Love for God. Jesus referred not just to paying taxes but to having a concern for one's heart and mind as well.

Relationship Between Morality and Community

Paul was the primary teacher in the Bible concerning the relationship between morality and the community. His Christ-based community had been established in Corinth but it was feared that this early Christian community might be destroyed if they didn't learn to work together. The behavior that he tried to encourage was strictly moral only because he believed that the success of the community depended upon it. In the book Acts, Paul's words are often characterized with appeals to Jesus as being the prime example for the people to follow. He often invokes "The name of our Lord Jesus Christ" to authorize the behavior in which he wants the Corinthians to engage.

Place of Mercy and Love

Jesus teachings on love and mercy are extensive in both his words and the example of his life. A famous parable that Jesus told of the Good Samaritan illustrated how a man who showed mercy on someone who others passed along the side of the road was a truly moral person. Jesus also said that "All the Law and the Prophets hang upon the Two Great Commandments, to love thy Lord God and to love thy neighbor."

The example of Jesus life is one that has many instances of both mercy and love. Jesus was said to have healed many people who were sick and dying. He ultimately sacrificed his own life in order to show others the way to Heaven.

Apparent Paradoxes in the Traditions

A paradox is something that seems to be contradictory and yet may nonetheless be true. In the Biblical tradition, one of the greatest paradoxes is thought to be the fact that a sinner is often in danger of falling into hell only by the result of his or her actions. The saint, however, is said to go to Heaven solely by the grace and power of God.

This seemingly contradictory belief that is present in the Biblical Tradition leaves several possibilities for reconciliation. One of these lies in the understanding of what it means to be a human being. By reflecting on one's own personal identity, a Christian may come to a new understanding of who they are and their life's purpose. They may begin to change and have an entirely new perception of who they are. From Jesus teachings, this seems to have been his greatest hope.

Moral Law: Epictetus, Aquinas, Hobbes, Locke, Jefferson, Kant, etc.

Philosophers continued to debate the idea of moral law for centuries after the establishment of the Greek and Biblical traditions. Epictetus was a Greek philosopher who continued the tradition of Greek philosophy in the first century after Jesus death. Later on, in the 1200's, St. Thomas Aquinas emerged as an important Christian philosopher who carried on the Biblical Tradition. Several hundred years later, during the time of the 1600's to the 1800's, there emerged some of the most important debates that now shape modern moral philosophy. One of the most important moral philosophers of this time period was a German philosopher named Immanuel Kant.

Besides the introduction of Kant's moral philosophy, an important debate which emerged amongst philosophers during this time was the idea of the social contract. The social contract is an agreement between two or more parties who commonly have differing or opposing interests. It is like a legal promise and it was the central concern of many philosophers of that day. Thomas Hobbes, John Locke, Jacques Rousseau and Thomas Jefferson emerged as some of the most important social contract theorists during this time and they were later joined by John Rawls in the 20th century.

The debate about moral law continued in the 20th century with important figures like Dr. Martin Luther King Jr. who activated a debate about civil rights. Also, Ralph Waldo Emerson and Henry David Thoreau introduced the idea of Transcendentalism into mainstream philosophy in the 1900's. All of these philosophers, from Epictetus to Thoreau, will be the focus of the next section on Moral Law.

The Enlightenment was a way of thinking which began developing in the 1800's. The main principle of the Enlightenment was that reason and rationality were the order of the world. Thinkers of the Enlightenment worked to end ignorance and superstition (especially as it related to the Catholic church) by presenting science and reason as the basis of morality. The basis of the Enlightenment was anything true could be proved by science or logic. One example of an Enlightenment thinker is Immanuel Kant. Kant argued that if reason could be used to explain all physical laws, then it could also explain all moral laws. For example, he believed that moral laws had to be universally applicable, and that would make them irrefutable. The physical law "triangles have three sides" applies both to individual triangles and triangles as a whole, and is therefore universal. However, the statement "I should steal all my food from others" is not universal, because it is illogical. If everyone were to steal their food from others, no one would be buying food for them to steal.

View of Human Nature

Epictetus carried on the Greek Tradition by introducing his students to two important concepts of human nature. These were the concepts of Prohairesis and Dihairesis. Prohairesis was what Epictetus called the distinguishing factor that separated human beings from all other creatures on the planet. It was considered to be the quality in humans that made them desire things or feel repelled by things. Dihairesis, on the other hand was the judgement itself that was made by a person's Prohairesis. Learning to distinguish between these two was very important.

Epictetus taught that good and evil existed only in our Prohairesis and that this was what basically constituted our human nature. Anyone who had thoroughly grasped these concepts and put them to use in their daily life would be better equipped to live the philosophic life and to find what Aristotle had called Eudaimonia.

Basis of Natural Law

When we talk about natural law in ethics, we are talking about the moral standards that determine our human behavior. We define right and wrong in terms of "the way we naturally are." It just makes sense for us to act this way. One example would be the natural law of wanting to be happy. This is just how we are made. If we believe in natural law, we believe that our moral standards should come from our human nature.

St. Thomas Aquinas is most well known for having a moral theory that was focused around the idea of natural law. For Thomas Aquinas, there were two main ideas that made up the natural law. The first was the idea that God was in the role of being the giver of the natural law. The second idea was that human beings were merely the receivers of this law.

A more important idea which Thomas Aquinas taught to his students was that natural law had an underlying basis. Natural law was just an aspect of a larger concept known as "Divine Providence." Thomas Aquinas believed that human beings were truly blessed or "lucky" to be in a position to learn about natural law from God. They didn't deserve it and they should therefore feel extremely grateful. This was the underlying basis of the natural law. Because of this, Aquinas thought that people should take advantage of the great opportunity to learn about natural law.

Principle of Double Effect

The principle of double effect is based on the idea that an action can simultaneously be both good and bad. One of the first to really examine this phenomenon was Thomas Aquinas. He addressed how an individual should approach a situation in which a good action would also yield a foreseeable bad result. Based on his theory there are several criteria by which such situations could be justified as moral despite the negative consequences. Firstly, the action in question must be either inherently good or inherently neutral. An act that is widely accepted as immoral should not be justified regardless of the good it might cause.

Secondly, a bad act cannot justify a good consequence. It must be a good act resulting in negative consequences. Thirdly, the good act and good consequences must be the motivation. A person who desires the negative consequences cannot reasonably justify their act as moral. Lastly, the good effect must be greater than or equal to the negative effect.

For example, the principle of double effect is often used to justifying giving pain relief medication to terminal patients, even though it may shorten their life expectancy. This is because the action (relieving pain) is inherently good. Furthermore, the relief of the patient's pain is the primary motivation for the act, not their quickened death. Therefore the motivation is primarily good, and the shortened life expectancy is simply a negative consequence. Also, many people typically view the relief of pain as equal to the negative effect of the shortened life. Therefore, based on Aquinas' four principles, the act can be considered moral.

 Metaethics

The field of metaethics is essentially the discussion behind the underlying principles of applied ethics. Metaethics seeks to examine and define ethical principles, reasoning, and standards, and to better understand them. For example, while applied ethics may consider the question "when is it right to lie?" from a metaethics standpoint the more important questions would be "what makes something right?" or "how is right defined?" Other examples of common metaethical questions are "what makes something good or bad?" or "what is justice?" By asking questions such as these, metaethics seeks to understand the underlying reasoning of the field of ethics.

Natural Rights and Duties

Natural rights are rights that exist independent of any government institution or ruler. These rights, if they do exist, would exist "no matter what." They would be universal. An example of a natural right is the right to be free. Immanuel Kant believed that people got their natural rights through reason.

Concerning duties, Immanuel Kant's philosophy became the most influential of his time. He presented a principle of morality which leads to four types of duties. These four duties fell under two main classes. The first class of duties were duties to oneself. The second class were duties to others. These two classes were then divided into two subtypes; perfect and imperfect duties. These divisions gave the four types of duties; perfect duties to oneself, imperfect duties to oneself, perfect duties to others and imperfect duties to others.

Perfect duties refer to specific kinds of actions. If you break a specific duty, it is considered to be morally blameworthy. In other words, you must do these "or else." Imperfect duties refer to general things and if you perform one of these, it is considered to be morally praiseworthy. In other words, you get "bonus points." An example of a perfect duty to oneself would be to "not kill yourself." An example of an imperfect duty to oneself might be to "improve your talents."

Relationship of Natural Law to Religious Belief

The relationship between natural law and religious belief is also something that was addressed in detail by St. Thomas Aquinas. Aquinas made a point of distinguishing between what he called Divine law and natural law. He said that natural law was only a subset of the larger Divine law and that Divine law could only be known through religious revelation. Divine law provided the ultimate purpose of man's life which was to have an intimate relationship with God.

In order to be clear about the differences between natural law and Divine law, he went into a lot of detail about what constituted natural law. Aquinas said that natural law was something that guided people to avoid doing anything that would prevent their natural ends. People's natural ends were determined according to their natural inclinations. He went into even more detail by explaining that all people had the same natural inclinations simply by being members of the same species. The three natural inclinations that he identified were self-preservation, reproduction (and/or care of offspring) and the use of reason to organize our lives. He said that the first inclination always took priority over the others and the second inclination always took priority over the third.

Source of Political Authority

All of the social contract theorists; Hobbes, Locke and Rousseau had a special interest in political theory. Hobbes believed that the main task of political society was to determine who should be the "person in charge" or the sovereign. This sovereign was then supposed to have absolute power and the citizens were supposed to obey all the time.

John Locke, however, believed that a legislative body should be empowered to determine the laws for the people. Rousseau believed that laws made by the legislature had the special requirement of having to address the common good of the people. He proposed methods for determining the common good but always put the people in charge as the main authority.

In terms of who should be the source of political authority then, there was a development in the political theory of these three philosophers. Hobbes prescribed a limited role of authority on the part of the people. John Locke gave the people more authority and Jacques Rousseau gave them the most authority. Rousseau may be most famously known for his statement "Man was born free, and everywhere he is in chains."

 Social Contract

Hobbes, Locke and Rousseau were the three main social contract theorists. For them, a social contract was an agreement between individuals, groups, government or a community which always benefited the people involved. Social contract theory has been the study of how to make the best kind of social contract. This determination often involved lengthy discussions about government and laws that supported a social contract between individuals. Of course, a contract wouldn't hold any weight if there wasn't a legal system and other institutions to back it up.

Besides the three main contract theorists, there were two others who were significant. John Rawls and Thomas Jefferson also had a lot to say on the idea of the social contract. The most recent of the social contract theorists is John Rawls who invented a theory around the social contract called "justice as fairness." Rawls' theory for social justice supports the idea of helping the poor and the less fortunate. Earlier in history, Thomas Jefferson had stressed the importance of inalienable rights for the individual which were similar to Kants "natural rights." The first two paragraphs of the Declaration of Independence now give a very clear statement of the doctrine of these rights laid down by Jefferson. Thomas Jefferson also supported a small government for the people, which was similar to John Locke's earlier system.

Relationship of Natural Law and Human Law

Human law is just a fancy term to describe the basic laws that are created by a government and are enforced by the police. Most people have a pretty good idea what the human law is in their country and they try to follow it just in order to stay out of trouble. Natural law, however, is a little more complicated and many people have different opinions about what the natural law is.

From review, we will remember that natural law is said to be the things that people think should be right or wrong based on our human nature or inclinations. It is also said that these things just "make sense" for us to follow them. Because there is a lot of debate about what these things are, only some of the ideas that come from natural law end up being instituted as human law. A legal case which revolved around the difference between natural law and human law might involve the amount of censorship that should be provided for certain "adult" material. Lawyers would debate how much of these materials are "natural" and how much are harmful and therefore should be illegal.

 Just War Theory

The classic Just-War Theory began in Christian theology. Saint Augustine is referred to as the first person to create a theory on the justifiability of war and justice. St. Thomas Aquinas revised Augustine's version, simplifying it and creating just three criteria for a just war: the war needed to be waged by a legitimate authority such as the state. This would represent the common good, peace for the sake of man. The second purpose is that war must have a good purpose, not for self-gain or simply for the exercise of power. There needed to a purpose such as restoring lost territory, goods, etc. Third, the war must be fought with the right intentions, to right a wrong, for ultimate peace.

Justifiability of Revolution or Civil Disobedience

In 1849, a very famous essay was written by a man who spent a night in jail for refusing to pay a tax. His name was Henry David Thoreau and the essay is called "Civil Disobedience." At the time, Thoreau believed that the money he was supposed to pay would be used to fund a war that he disagreed with. He believed the Mexican War would lead to the increase of slave territory in the United States and he thought that it was immoral.

Thoreau famously wrote, "I heartily accept the motto, 'That government is best which governs least'; and I should like to see it acted up to more rapidly and systematically. Carried out, it finally amounts to this, which also I believe--That government is best which governs not at all; and when men are prepared for it, that will be the kind of government which they will have."

Years later, may famous revolutionaries were inspired by Thoreau's words and actions. Rosa Parks was a famous civil rights activist who was arrested for Civil Disobedience in 1955. Martin Luther King Jr. led a peaceful civil rights movement in the United States and Mahatma Gandhi helped lead India out from under the oppression of the British occupation.

Equality and Liberty

Thomas Jefferson once said "The tree of liberty must be refreshed from time to time with the blood of patriots and tyrants." Although philosophers have debated the truths of equality and liberty for centuries, it has oftentimes been the case that people have died prematurely for their beliefs. This has never been more true than in cases of people who stood up for the belief in equality and liberty. In many cases, the death of great activists has contributed to the increase of consciousness for the many people who are left behind. This was certainly been the case for Dr. Martin Luther King Jr. who was assassinated in 1968.

Concerning the idea of equality, Dr. Martin Luther King once said "I have a dream that one day on the red hills of Georgia, the sons of former slaves and the sons of former slave owners will be able to sit together at the table of brotherhood." Although the loss of Dr. King was very tragic, it has not been uncommon to see great thinkers like this suffer an untimely death.

Mahatma Gandhi was another example of this kind of tragic loss. The humor of these great minds has never been without its spark; however, as one of the most influential activists in history, Mahatma Gandhi once made this humorous remark in reference to the importance of equality: "I believe in equality for everyone, except reporters and photographers!"

Deontological vs. Consequential Moral Frameworks

Consequentialism is the ethical theory that holds the consequences of a particular action to be the basis for a moral judgement about that action. A morally right action would be an action which creates good consequences.

Immanuel Kant was strongly against Consequentialism. Instead, he presented another form of ethics known as Deontological ethics. This is the theory that decisions should be made solely or primarily by considering one's duties and the rights of others. Deontology says that there are basic inherent obligations that people have. It gives a set of defined principles that never change. Kant believed that particular kinds of acts are morally wrong because they are inconsistent with a person's status as free and rational.

Hypothetical and Categorical Imperatives

Immanuel Kant thought that morality could be summed up in just one ultimate principle. Once this principle was established, all the other duties and obligations could then be determined according to that principle. The ultimate principle that he thought would satisfy this need was called the Categorical Imperative.

For Kant, there were actually two types of imperatives but only one of them could serve as an ultimate principle. A hypothetical imperative would only dictate actions in particular circumstances. An example would be if someone were hungry, the hypothetical imperative would dictate that they should stop at a restaurant and eat. A categorical imperative, however, would be an absolute requirement that exerts its authority in all circumstances. It was both required and justified as what Kant referred to as "an end in itself." The first formulation of Kant's Categorical Imperative reads as; "Act only according to that maxim by which you can, at the same time, will that it would become a universal law."

Good Will and Duty for its Own Sake

The idea of doing something for its own sake is central to Kant's moral philosophy. Kant believed that it was a neutral consequence whether something turned out to be good in the long run. The important thing was to do the right thing regardless of the results. He thought that all people had a duty to carry out certain things simply because these things were good "in and of themselves." That was the basis of Kant's morality. Good actions are good just for their own sake, not because they do or don't result in something afterwards.

Kant believed that his Categorical Imperative was the statement that could be used as a reference for all duties that were to be carried out as moral actions. Because the results of an act are not what make them good, the source was simply the underlying maxim that was contained in the Categorical Imperative.

 ## Persons as Ends in Themselves Not as Means Only

Yet another important idea that was presented by Immanuel Kant's theory of moral law was that people should always be treated as "ends in themselves." When we have relationships with others, we have a choice to either use people for our own personal gains or to treat them with respect. The respect we showed to others would be such that they were considered to be an end in themselves. They had their own individual worth apart from us. They wanted to be free just like us and should be treated that way because of the Categorical Imperative.

Kant believed that freedom was the greatest value that people had. If a person were to act according to the Categorical Imperative, he or she would have to treat other people in such a way as to encourage and allow for their freedom. This was because freedom was considered by Kant to be a universal maxim and it fit perfectly within the principle of the Categorical Imperative.

 ## Loyalty and Virtue

Loyalty is often considered to be a secondary virtue because its value is often determined according to where a person chooses to place their loyalty. Many systems of government have sought to encourage loyalty in their people and the philosophy of Jacques Rousseau has served to encourage this end as well.

Although Rousseau spoke in favor of loyalty, he also said that there should be no independent associations within the state because they would only hurt that state over time. It was the allegiance to private, local groups that Rousseau saw as an eventual threat to people's freedom. He especially noted the different religious groups as likely to erode the loyalty of the people to their country. Although he believed in the power of the people, he also felt that the people should not form these independent groups. It was for this reason that Rousseau made his famous statement "Man was born free, and everywhere he is in chains."

Ironically, Rousseau's ideas have more often been promoted by totalitarian governments rather than being respected in the way he would have liked. Although he would have preferred that individuals respect his ideas and refrain from independent associations on their own, another tendency in people has often been the case. Thomas Jefferson saw this tendency in people and rather than preventing it, he encouraged it.

In a democracy, different groups with different beliefs are encouraged. This is because Thomas Jefferson believed that these independent associations would actually help to create a larger national loyalty rather than degrade it. This is a debate that still goes on today in many countries and between many individuals.

 Vices

A common way of discussing the ethical traits of a person is in terms of their virtues and vices. Virtues are the good character traits that an individual possess. Vices, on the other hand, are the negative traits. The term vice is used to describe the shortcomings or immoral traits that a person possesses. For example, while an individual could possess the virtue of honesty, another may possess the vices of dishonesty, deceitfulness, recklessness, and so forth. Aristotle was known for his study of virtues and vices. He argued that any virtue could become a vice if taken too far, or if not fully developed. For example, consider the virtue of courage. If taken too far it could lead an individual to be overly rash. On the other hand, if not fully developed, courage gives way to cowardice. According to Aristotle, balance is essential.

Relationship of Morality to Self-Interest and Happiness

Returning to the earlier teachings of the Greeks and Epictetus, it was Epictetus belief that the natural instinct of man was toward self-preservation and his own self-interest. Regardless of this, however, Epictetus thought that individual men were incapable of securing their own self-interests unless they contributed to the overall welfare of others. He believed that men were tied by the laws of nature and the entire fabric of the universe. It was therefore necessary, in order to achieve happiness, that people embrace the entire world and the will of nature into their view. They must never indulge in anger or jealousy or envy because, in this way, they would not grow into what Epictetus called "the mind of God."

Even though self-interest was the natural instinct, Epictetus believed that happiness could not be obtained without morality. Through morality and incorporating the larger picture of things into one's world view, a person could finally achieve happiness.

Conceptions of Justice

In 1971, John Rawls published *A Theory of Justice*, which addresses an interesting theory concerning social contracts. It has sparked endless debate in the past few decades about which conception of justice is best. Rawls specific theory is known as the "Justice as Fairness" theory and it introduces two famous principles known as the **liberty principle** and the **difference principle**. The liberty principle basically says that you can't be 100% free until everyone else is 100% free. The difference principle says that only the poor and disadvantaged should benefit from any special treatment to individuals.

Rawls argues that his principles are true because anybody who didn't know who was going to be rich and who was going to be poor, would always choose these policies just to be safe. They were based on the idea that anyone who was ignorant of individual status, would always choose this way.

Fairness and Distributive Justice

In his "Justice as Fairness" theory, John Rawls is trying to solve the problem of distributive justice. Distributive justice refers to how much is the right amount of goods that should be distributed to people based on the outcome or consequences of the decision.

Distributive justice is part of a consequentialist theory because it focuses on outcomes. Similar to Kant, Rawls was against consequentialism and he supported Kant's deontological theory of morality instead. Since distributive justice concentrated on just outcomes and had a tendency to look like a consequentialist theory, Rawls instead tried to focus his "Justice as Fairness" theory on another kind of justice known as procedural justice. Procedural justice concentrated on just processes rather than just outcomes.

Euthanasia

Euthanasia is a term associated with mercy killing, allowing someone to die, physician assisted suicide, and other such situations. Euthanasia generally does not apply to situations where a patient is pronounced brain dead, because medically, they are no longer alive. There are two types of euthanasia, active and passive. Active euthanasia is when a person actually does something to end a patient's life, such as injecting with poison, or causing a lethal overdose of prescribed medications.

Physician assisted suicide and mercy killing fall under this category. Passive euthanasia is when medical treatment is withheld. For example, "do not resuscitate" orders, or DNR's, are considered a form of passive euthanasia (a DNR is a legal document in which a patient states that they do not want to be revived if their heart or lungs stop working), as is taking a person off life support. Dr. Jack Kevorkian was one of the most well known advocates of physician assisted suicide and helped to end the lives of over 100 patients, despite legal orders and restrictions.

Suicide can be contrasted with euthanasia. The philosopher John Locke had a unique view on suicide. He believed that humans belong to God, and because of this, it was His (God's) right to determine how long a person lives. He believed that it was not a person's right to commit suicide. However, there were also cases in which he believed it to be acceptable. He believed it justified if it served a bigger purpose than just suicide. For example, in his *Treatise* he implies that for prisoner's of war to commit suicide is justified if they are being treated too harshly.

Consequential Ethics: Epicurus, Bentham, Mill

As we discussed earlier, Consequentialism is based on the theory that the consequences of a particular action are the basis for how to determine right and wrong. A morally right action is something that results in good consequences. The previous forms of ethics that we have discussed have been Virtue ethics, as in the case of Plato, Aristotle or Aquinas and Deontological ethics as in the case of Immanuel Kant. Deontological ethics emphasized the type of action rather than the consequences. Virtue ethics focused on the character and inclinations of the person involved.

In Consequential ethics, we now focus entirely on the consequences of an action in order to determine whether it is right or wrong. Three major proponents of consequential ethics were The Greek philosopher Epicurus and the English philosophers Jeremy Bentham and John Stuart Mill.

Consequential vs. Deontological Moral Frameworks

Utilitarianism is the most popular form of consequential ethics and it was started by the English philosopher John Stuart Mill. In his book, he explained the theory of Utilitarianism which stated that actions were right in as much as they tend to promote happiness and they were wrong when they tended to produce the opposite. By "happiness" Mill made sure to clarify that he meant both intellectual and sensual pleasures. He said that people have a sense of dignity which makes them prefer intellectual pleasures over sensual pleasures.

Mill was against Deontological ethics and criticized Immanuel Kant's Categorical Imperative. He said that the Categorical Imperative was really just a utilitarianism theory in disguise. To him, it still seemed that the Categorical Imperative would require calculating the good or bad consequences of an action to determine the rightness or wrongness of that action.

Hedonism and Kinds of Pleasure

Hedonism is the belief that happiness is obtained through the pleasures of the senses. Jeremy Bentham and John Stuart Mill both developed their utilitarian philosophies around the idea of hedonism but they each defined "pleasure" in a different way. Bentham believed that the value of a sensual pleasure could be measured as an amount or a quantity and could be given ratings according to its length of time and its intensity. In this way, his ethics was based around only trying to obtain the greatest amount of sensory pleasure. John Stuart Mill, however, thought sensory pleasures should be categorized more in terms of their quality or "level" rather than their amount.

He explained that there were lower quality pleasures and higher quality pleasures and ethics was a matter of pursuing the higher quality sensual pleasures rather than the lower. Epicurus defined pleasure so as to distinguish it entirely from the senses and instead categorize it more as a function of the mind. For Epicurus, the only pleasures that really brought happiness were defined as "refined" pleasures as opposed to coarse pleasures which came from the body. For Epicurus, the highest pleasure a person could reach was the pleasure of tranquility. This could be obtained only by eliminating all of a person's simple desires and then obtaining peace.

Self-Interest or Prudence and the Common Good

Even though Epicurus distinguished his idea of pleasure as being a pleasure of the mind, he was still opposed by his earlier Greek predecessors like Plato and Aristotle. This was because he insisted that virtue was only good for obtaining one's own self-interest and it didn't have any real value on its own. Plato and Aristotle had often given praise to the virtues just for their own sake. Epicurus, however, was a consequentialist and thought that all virtues were just important in terms of what consequences they brought. He said that they were all forms of something called "prudence."

For Epicurus, virtues or "prudence" were a way of calculating what was is in a person's own best interest and then making it possible to obtain their own happiness. One's own happiness was really the only true value. The "common good" that Plato and Socrates had often spoken of only amounted to another form of prudence for Epicurus. The common good was a secondary consideration that was only good for obtaining one's own self-interest.

Joel Feinberg

Joel Feinberg was an American philosopher of the 20th century. He was well known for his support of the ethical theories of psychological egoism. Psychological egoism is a theory which argues that people always act according to their own best interests.

According to Feinberg, humans are incapable of acting in any other way. In essence, every choice that an individual makes shows what their priorities are and what is most important to them. A person may wish to relax at home, but also to make money. Therefore, by going to work they are showing what is most important to them – making money. The theory of psychological egoism argues that even choices which may initially appear selfless are motivated by underlying self-interested motives. For example, they could be motivated by a desire to feel heroic, or a desire for attention. It's important to understand, however, that this philosophy does not advocate egoism a prescriptive theory of how decisions should be made. Rather it simply notes it as the method by which they are made.

Friedrich Nietzsche

Friedrich Nietzsche was a German philosopher of the 19th century. He is widely known for his encouragement for individuals to become what you are. In advocating this, he rejected notions that would lead a person beyond their sphere of existence – including belief in God or other powers transcending this life. Many times in his writings he argued against traditional notions of Christianity, instead claiming God to be dead. Nietzsche is also one of few historical philosophers to advocate the theory of Nihilism.

Nihilism is a radical theory which rejects all notions of morality, religious principles, and social order. It is essentially the idea that all things are meaningless. Nietzsche argued that if one examines the sum of existence, no amount of religious ideology or morality will have any lasting effect. In other words, decisions and beliefs are pointless because in the end nothing relevant really changes as a result. Although Nietzsche's writings are often contradictory and unclear, he nonetheless had an important influence on philosophical thought of the 19th and 20th centuries. Nietzsche suffered a collapse and was mentally incapacitated for the last ten years of his life.

Principle of Utility or Greatest Happiness Principle

Jeremy Bentham's "principle of utility" first stated that pleasure and pain were the only true absolutes in the entire world and that, because of this, the only thing that could be called "good" was the thing that brought the greatest amount of happiness to the greatest number of people. Later on, Bentham changed his "principle of utility" to simply be called the "greatest happiness principle."

Felicific Calculus

Felicific Calculus was a method invented by Jeremy Bentham for calculating the total amount of pleasure and pain that comes from an action. In this way a person could accurately determine the good or bad consequences of an action. Bentham thought that a person should consider the intensity and duration as well as other things. They should determine how certain they were about the consequences and also how close the consequences would be to the action itself. Even more considerations included how often the consequences would occur from just one action and what the chances were that it would be followed by others. The number of persons affected was also a consideration and alternative courses of action had to be taken into consideration. Bentham thought that his calculus could be used to determine penalties for crimes and appropriate sentences as well.

Conscience and External Sanctions of Morality

John Stuart Mill discussed the concept of external sanctions in his philosophy. He defined external sanctions as the natural desire that people had to please others. People just wanted to be liked by others and nobody wished to be disliked. Mill also said this was also true in terms of a natural belief that anyone might have in God. Those people would naturally want God to be pleased with them and would avoid God's displeasure. Eventually, these desires developed in people to create a general feeling of conscience in a person.

Apart from all these facts, John Stuart Mill still held firm on his claim that natural desires were all basically selfish desires on the part of human beings. People only did things for others or for God in order to feel good about themselves. Mill thought that the ideas of conscience and external sanctions fit perfectly into his theory of Utilitarianism.

Self-Regarding and Other Regarding Conduct

In order to clarify his philosophy even further John Stuart Mill also explained a distinction between self-regarding conduct and other-regarding conduct. Self-regarding concept was considered to be the actions that affect only the person who is carrying them out. If a person chooses to drink cherry soda instead of regular soda, this is his or her own business and doesn't affect anyone else. Other-regarding conduct however is the set of actions that do affect others. It was Mill's intention to make this distinction in order to make the claim that society should never interfere with a person's self-regarding conduct.

An obvious problem with Mill's distinction arose when it was suggested that there wasn't any real distinction between what Mill had called self-regarding conduct and what he called other-regarding conduct. Everything a person did affected others in a least some small degree. Mill responded to this saying that the ultimate distinction was in an action that violated the other person's obligations that they had to themselves to find happiness. This ultimate distinction showed that it would be immoral only because it prevented others from being happy.

Individual Liberty and the Limits of the State's Authority

Having made the distinction about what was right and wrong, Mill went on to apply his ideas to the government. He said "The only purpose for which power can be rightfully exercised over any member of a civilized community, against his will, is to prevent harm to others." Mill thought that the government interfering with the freedom of an individual was almost never acceptable. He thought that governments should never be allowed to "limit private thoughts and feelings, public expression, individual tastes, the pursuit to live happily or the association of like-minded individuals with each other."

Mill also famously said "No society is truly free unless its individual citizens are permitted to take care of themselves."

A pacifist is a person who is opposed to violence and war of any kind. Pacifists apply to ethics because of programs such as drafting. It has been questioned if it is unethical to force a person who is a pacifist to fight in wars.

Feminist Ethics

The goal of feminism is complete equality between women and men. This applies to political, social, and economic situations. Feminism is an ethical question because there is no scientific basis to believe that women are not equal to men. However, in the past, women were considered the inferior gender. The feminist movement is an attempt to ensure that there isn't unethical or unfair treatment of women. For example, woman suffrage was the first goal of the early feminist movement. They felt women were perfectly capable of voting, and that it was unfair that they weren't allowed to. Eventually that type of political inequality was corrected.

Although many people think of feminist ethics as having just begun in the 1960's, this is certainly not the case. There were many eighteenth and nineteenth-century philosophers such as Mary Wollstonecraft and John Stuart Mill who discussed the specific issues of women's morality many years ago. These kinds of discussions even went back as far as St. Thomas Aquinas and Aristotle. Philosophers have discussed the ideas about women's psychological traits and social roles for centuries. In those early days, Aristotle and Aquinas even suggested that moral virtues and psychological traits were connected with a person's physiology and that men and women might show different moral virtues in addition to having different psychological traits.

Although feminist ethics has a long tradition, it has become more prominent in the past several decades with names like Carol Gilligan and Lawrence Kohlberg taking center stage. These two modern philosophers will be the focus of this brief section on feminist ethics.

These ethical discussions have led to affirmative action. Affirmative action is a principle of benefiting underrepresented groups by taking factors such as race, gender, or religion into account in business and educational settings. For example, universities that practice affirmative action actively recruit and admit people of minority races.

Ayn Rand

Ayn Rand is an author most well known for two of her books: *The Fountainhead* and *Atlas Shrugged*. However, in addition to her career as a writer Ayn Rand is also an advocate of the ethical model that she has developed which she calls objectivism. Rand argues that principles of reality, reason, and free will are what determine the morality of an action.

In terms of reality, objectivism claims that reality is absolute. Rand rejects any amount of subjectivity in determining truth. Instead, she argues that truth is unchanging and fixed. No amount of wishing or desire by an individual can change the realities of a situation, and there is no deity that sets the terms of existence. According to objectivism, nature is the sum of existence. The second principle, reason, describes the importance of logic and reason. Because all truths are fixed, it is both possible and necessary to discover them. Knowledge is the means of human progression and the arbiter of morality. Lastly, Rand strongly defends the principles of free will – that individuals must have the right and ability to act for themselves. For this reason, Rand is also a strong advocate of total capitalism.

Jane English

Jane English is a philosopher well known for her feminist and gender related theories. She is an advocate of women's rights and gender equality. English is particularly known for her theories relating to abortion. In her book *Abortion and the Concept of a Person* English argues that whether or not a fetus constitutes a person is irrelevant when considering abortion. English states that if the fetus can be considered a person there are still cases in which abortion is justified. Furthermore, English argues that even if the fetus cannot be considered a person there are cases in which abortion is not justified. This claim is related to the treatment of animals. Although animals are not people, mistreating them is still immoral. English proposed that there are many different factors which affect the morality of abortion.

Religious Belief Systems

While other approaches take on a more objective view of religion, not passing judgment on the beliefs themselves, a theologian questions the validity of the belief system.

They want to know if the beliefs are true or false and why people respond to those beliefs. The study from this point of view is always grounded in religious tradition.

Taking a theological viewpoint means taking a close look at the ethics and acts of worship of a religion. Often a theologian will investigate the religion with the idea that a belief is true, and then the scientist explores the beliefs more fully. He or she will then relate the faith to the world around him or her and apply it to world situations.

Theologists tend to look at religion from a variety of angles. They may look at it from a critically analytical point of view or a historical point of view. There is also the systematic point of view in the attributes of the religion. Finally, there is the practical point of view that tends to look at the practical application of religion. Often, though, these approaches are combined to give theologians a deeper understanding of the religion.

Primal Religions

Primal religions may be relegated by those in "developed" countries as nonsense, but in truth many tribes are significantly more religious that those in other societies. They live closer to the land, where they are at the mercy of nature and death, so they tend to feel that they are surrounded by evil. They have a strong understanding that they are surrounded by an invisible power, and each society has constructed a religious system that explains and connects them to this power.

This link means that primal religions have a way of meeting the needs of the people. In primal religions, the people tend to have a sense of human nature, and understanding of the fragility of life, and a dependence on the spirit world. The term "primal" is meant to show that these religions came before the "universal religions" like Christianity or Hinduism. These religions have been subject to demeaning terms like "heathen," "animistic," "savage," or "primitive," and those terms tend to be offensive to those that practice it.

Primal religions tend to have some common characteristics. There is often a strong belief in a spirit world where there are powers greater than those of man. Most of these religions contain a belief that we are not alone. This spirit power tends to be in everything and everyone, though in some religions it can be concentrated in one person. In other primal religions, the spirit powers are contained in Gods, although there are several primal religions that are monotheistic. Monotheistic means that they only believe in one God.

Another common characteristic in primal religions is the belief in the living dead. They believe that the dead communicate with the living, and that the ancestral spirits must be honored. Often this is considered "ancestor worship."

While ancestor worship is common, so is the dependence on myths. Most primal religions are based upon myths, or complicated stories that exhibit a religion's theology and philosophy. They also rely on dreams and visions to guide a person or community.

Rituals are an important characteristic of primal religions. For many, the New Year involves some of the most important rituals. These rituals often combine the myth and an act of worship. Sometimes they culminate in a great festival or sacrifice.

Finally, most of these primal religions need a central figure to help with the activities and rituals. They are often referred to as a "medicine man." The medicine men tend to fill a number of roles like priest, healer, diviner, shaman, or medium. A shaman is a priest, someone that deals with the spirits and spirit world. It is a broad term that includes healers, sorcerers, priests, exorcists, etc.

Native North American Traditions

One of the areas that are seeing resurgence in primal beliefs is in the Native North American culture. For a while, the influence of Western Civilization had discredited and shunned the beliefs of these native peoples. However, with the recent lack of consideration for the environment, community, and spirituality, many of these cultures are turning back to their religious roots.

The native people of North America have a wisdom rooted in the past. They have a strong emphasis placed on the teaching of the ancients. They may have a One Great Spirit. For the Inuit people of Southeast Alaska, the closest thing they have to One Great Spirit is the Old Woman who lived under the sea.

In many Native American mythologies they have a coyote or raven known as "the trickster" who acts as a central figure in their folk stories.

The Inuit people practiced Shamanism with an underlying animist principle. This principle is also common in North American tribes, as it asserts that everything has a form of spirit, which can be influenced by supernatural entities. They acknowledged the fragility of humanity, like many other Native North American cultures. They believed that their existence was based entirely on the consumption of souls, animal souls that were thought to be equal to humans, and so they gave great respect to the animals they hunted.

The Lakota is another North American culture that practices shamanism, but they do have One Great Spirit called Wakan Tanka. They place a lot of emphasis on visions and dreams. They have a number of rituals that honor the spirits in the things that surround them.

They often perform rites of passage that encourage visions, and it is said that a Lakota boy cannot become a man until he has a vision. They have a strong idea of good and bad in the world, and they do recognize that there is a salvation.

Lakota are also known for their sundance, a traditional ceremony representing life and rebirth. The main ceremony is four days long, once a year. The day before the sundance begins a tree is cottonwood tree is selected as it is sacred to the Lakota. It is sacred for two reasons. The first, it is the tree that showed the Lakota how to make a tipi. Also, if you cut an upper limb crosswise, it will show inside a perfect five pointed star, which represents the presence Great Spirit. On the third day, those men who have pledged to pierce themselves do so in ceremony. This is their flesh sacrifice representing sacrifice for their tribe.

While the Lakota have their Great Spirit, and the Inuit their animist principles, the Hopi worship Kokopelli, the humpbacked flutist that took part in weddings and gave fetuses to pregnant women. The Hopi also have a strong belief in salvation and the afterlife. They believe that good people go west and become kachinas.

Social Dharma

There are two main concepts in classical Hinduism – Karma and Dharma. Karma is often referred to as a person's actions, which can be defined a good or bad. These actions would influence a person's destiny. Therefore, dharma came to play as religious duty and a social order required by religious law. Responsible action was definable by one's class, so social dharma was created, and even the Bhagavad-Gita deems it wrong to try and fulfill someone else's dharma. In Hinduism, ethical pursuits were all relative except for that which released the person from the cycle of rebirth. Many of the rules of dharma are outlined in the Laws of Manu.

There are four separate orders in Hinduism's social dharma. There is the student, householder, hermit, and ascetic. Each order has a specific dharma. In Hinduism the ritual acts of an order and ethics are combined. Today, Hindus place more emphasis on progress than time cycles. They tend to have more a focus on things like being truthful, kind, and loving while still retaining the goal of the common good.

David Gauthier

David Gauthier is a Canadian philosopher born in 1932. He is most known for developing a contractarian theory of ethics which has come to be called morals by agreement. As a contractarian philosophy, the theory of morals by agreement begins with a basic belief in social contracts.

In other words, the theory argues that because people tend to have opposing interests and beliefs, the most benefit to the collective human family is to be gained through cooperation and the formation of social contracts. Gauthier notes that, despite these contracts, individual advantages are typically gained at the expense of others. Gauthier argues that individuals should not worsen the situation of others for their own betterment, but rather that the best outcome is the one which creates the least amount of concession in the collective sense. In other words, the most moral outcome is the one that results in the least overall suffering. The greatest criticisms of Gauthier's theories are that it relies on the existence of bargaining capacity, and that it requires that all participants be willing to make some level of concession rather than seek their own gain in some situations.

Critique of Standard Ethics

Before focusing on the more modern conceptions of feminist ethics, it will serve to note that the eighteenth-century philosophers like Mary Wollstonecraft generally thought that men's and women's moralities were basically the same. This has not been the case in more modern conceptions. Proponents of feminine approaches to ethics like Carol Gilligan, have stressed that traditional moral theories were wrong because that they trivialized some of the most important qualities that women possess.

Carol Gilligan created much of her philosophy as a reaction to the Freudian notion that men had a well-developed moral sense but women did not. According to Gilligan, Freud was simply one of many western psychologists and philosophers who have seen women's moral inferiority where, in Gilligan's estimation, they should have instead seen a moral difference.

Gilligan focuses much of her criticism on her former mentor and teacher named Lawrence Kohlberg. Kohlberg thought that moral development was a six-stage process. Although Gilligan agreed that a six-stage process was an appealing idea, she didn't think it was true.

Alternative Visions – Care Ethic and Ethic of Trust

Carol Gilligan thought that women followed a different course than men in their moral development. Women didn't think in terms of "justice" and "rights." Instead, they thought in terms of "care" and "trust." Women were more concerned with maintaining relationships and taking care of people. Over the past two decades, Care Ethics has gained important ground as a more legitimate ethical approach for women. In recent years it has even gone beyond psychology and philosophy into the field of medicine where it is used to teach nursing ethics. Carol Gilligan has made a very significant contribution to the ongoing development of feminist ethics.

Many believe that men and women have distinct approaches and views of the world, and of ethics. Ethics of care is also known as the female view on ethics. While male ethics (ethics of justice) center on justice and independence, the ethics of care center on ideals such as generosity, harmony, and relationships. Another known for their support of the ethics of care is Rita Manning. She believes that the most important thing in how a person perceives ethics is their relationships with other people. She believes people to be "spiritually" bound to look after people they are related to.

Medical Ethics

Ethics in medicine include six main areas:

- Beneficence - acting in the best interest of the patient.
- Non-maleficence - do no harm.
- Autonomy - allowing the right to refuse treatment.
- Justice - fairness and equality in treatment.
- Dignity - patient's right to dignity.
- Truthfulness and honesty - informed consent.

Stem cells are cells which have the potential to become any type of cell. The adult body makes a type of stem cell which has the potential to become certain types of different cells, but cells which make up the very early embryo (5-7 days old) develop into many different types of cells. There is much controversy surrounding the research of these types of cells because extracting stem cells from a 5-7 day old embryo kills it. On the other hand, adult stem cells are less effective, more costly to procure, and harder to work with. Stem cell research could prove to be the cure for disabling diseases such as Alzheimer's, diabetes, and Parkinson's disease.

Sample Test Questions
Section 1: Ethical Traditions

1) Which of the following philosophers started the Peripatetic School?

   A) Thucydides
   B) Plato
   C) Aristotle
   D) Plotinus

The correct answer is C:) Aristotle.

2) Socrates was accused of which of these crimes?

   A) Murder
   B) Making slanderous and false accusations
   C) Threatening the government
   D) Corrupting the youth

The correct answer is D:) Corrupting the youth.

3) Plato believed which of these to be true about virtue and self-interest?

   A) Everybody always chooses to do the virtuous thing.
   B) You can't be virtuous if you have self-interest.
   C) People sometimes choose to do non-virtuous things.
   D) Some people do things without any self-interest.

The correct answer is A:) Everybody always chooses to do the virtuous thing.

4) Plotinus First Principle is best expressed through which two ideas?

   A) Virtue and Happiness
   B) Being and The Good
   C) Unity and Oneness
   D) Virtue and The Soul

The correct answer is C:) Unity and Oneness.

5) Thrasymachus statements express which two modern belief systems?

   A) Moral Skepticism and Relativism
   B) Self-Interest and Dominant Politics
   C) Punitive Justice and Force
   D) Modernism and Relative Skepticism

The correct answer is A:) Moral Skepticism and Relativism.

6) The Doctrine of the Mean was created by which philosopher?

   A) Socrates
   B) Plato
   C) Aristotle
   D) Plotinus

The correct answer is C:) Aristotle.

7) In Plato's cave, the normal objects that we see each day are symbolized by what?

   A) Dreams
   B) Walls
   C) Rocks
   D) Shadows

The correct answer is D:) Shadows.

8) The Doctrine of the Mean can be used for which purpose?

   A) Calculating how virtuous we are.
   B) Determining how much is right for us.
   C) Determining who is nice and who is mean.
   D) Calculating a mathematical average.

The correct answer is B:) Determining how much is right for us.

9) The type of 'mean' that falls between two extremes is which of the following?

   A) Relative mean
   B) Virtuous mean
   C) Moderate mean
   D) Absolute mean

The correct answer is D:) Absolute mean.

10) How were Jacob and Abraham related?

   A) Jacob was the first-born son of Abraham.
   B) Abraham was Jacob's ancestor.
   C) Jacob and Abraham were brothers.
   D) Jacob was Abraham's father.

The correct answer is B:) Abraham was Jacob's ancestor.

11) The covenant in the Bible refers to which promise?

   A) Abraham's promise to Jacob
   B) God's promise to Jacob
   C) Jacob's promise to Abraham
   D) God's promise to Abraham

The correct answer is D:) God's promise to Abraham.

12) A paradox is which of the following?

   A) Something that seems false because it is contradictory.
   B) Something that seems to be contradictory but may be true.
   C) Something that is contradictory but seems to be true.
   D) Something that is true but seems to be contradictory.

The correct answer is B:) Something that seems to be contradictory but may be true.

13) According to Aquinas, the basis of natural law is which of the following?

   A) God
   B) Divine Providence
   C) The way we naturally are
   D) Human nature

The correct answer is C:) The way we naturally are.

14) The two classes of duties, according to Kant, are which of the following?

   A) Perfect duties and imperfect duties.
   B) Perfect duties to oneself and imperfect duties to oneself.
   C) Duties to oneself and duties to others.
   D) Perfect duties to others and imperfect duties to others.

The correct answer is C:) Duties to oneself and duties to others.

15) Aquinas three natural inclinations are which of the following?

   A) Inclinations to self-preservation, reproduction and reason.
   B) Inclinations to Divine law, natural law and self-preservation.
   C) Inclinations to self-preservation, reproduction and care of offspring.
   D) Inclinations to sovereign rule, legislative rule and rule by the people.

The correct answer is A:) Inclinations to self-preservation, reproduction and reason.

16) The power given to the people increased according to which order of philosophers?

   A) Hobbes, Rousseau, Locke
   B) Locke, Rousseau, Hobbes
   C) Locke, Jefferson, Hobbes
   D) Hobbes, Locke, Rousseau

The correct answer is D:) Hobbes, Locke, Rousseau.

17) The first two paragraphs of the Declaration of Independence give an account of what?

   A) Social justice
   B) Inalienable rights
   C) Justice as fairness
   D) Natural rights

The correct answer is B:) Inalienable rights.

18) Who said "government is best which governs not at all"?

   A) Thomas Jefferson
   B) Mahatma Gandhi
   C) Dr. Martin Luther King
   D) Henry David Thoreau

The correct answer is D:) Henry David Thoreau.

19) Rousseau believed which of the following?

   A) Totalitarianism was the best kind of government.
   B) People could have individual groups and still be loyal to their country.
   C) People were hurting themselves by making independent associations.
   D) Loyalty to one's country was shameful.

The correct answer is C:) People were hurting themselves by making independent associations.

20) John Rawls invented his two principles on what basis?

   A) He wanted to help the poor and disadvantaged.
   B) Everyone would choose these principles if they were ignorant of individual status.
   C) These principles naturally follow from the definition of justice.
   D) He believed these principles would establish fairness.

The correct answer is B:) Everyone would choose these principles if they were ignorant of individual status.

21) John Rawls supported which philosopher's theory of morality?

   A) Jacques Rousseau
   B) Thomas Hobbes
   C) Immanuel Kant
   D) John Locke

The correct answer is C:) Immanuel Kant.

22) Three virtue ethicists that we have discussed so far are which of the following?

   A) Epicurus, Bentham and Mill
   B) Epicurus, Plato and Aristotle
   C) Plato, Aristotle and Aquinas
   D) Plato, Aristotle and Kant

The correct answer is C:) Plato, Aristotle and Aquinas.

23) Mill said what about Kant's Categorical Imperative?

   A) The Categorical Imperative was false.
   B) The Categorical Imperative was the same as Utilitarianism.
   C) The Categorical Imperative was true.
   D) The Categorical Imperative was only Deontological.

The correct answer is B:) The Categorical Imperative was the same as Utilitarianism.

24) Utilitarianism states which of the following?

   A) Actions were right according to their own nature.
   B) Actions were right when they promoted happiness.
   C) Actions were right when the person performing them was virtuous.
   D) Actions were right when the served the common good.

The correct answer is B:) Actions were right when they promoted happiness.

25) Epicurus thought which of the following?

   A) Prudence came from developing ones virtue.
   B) Prudence was the highest virtue possible.
   C) Prudence was one of the many virtues.
   D) Virtues were all forms of prudence.

The correct answer is D:) Virtues were all forms of prudence.

26) Three considerations in Felicific Calculus were which of the following?

   A) Intensity, duration and certainty.
   B) Pleasure, pain and activity.
   C) Good consequences, bad consequences and activity.
   D) Number of people affected, alternative courses and activity.

The correct answer is A:) Intensity, duration and certainty.

27) Mill believed that people naturally wanted to be liked by whom?

   A) God and family
   B) Family and others
   C) God and others
   D) Themselves and others

The correct answer is C:) God and others.

28) The ultimate distinction between self-regarding actions and other-regarding actions is what?

   A) Whether it affects another person.
   B) If the person has any regard for another person.
   C) If the person has regard for themselves.
   D) If they violate to the other persons obligations to themselves.

The correct answer is D:) If they violate to the other persons obligations to themselves.

29) According to Mill, the only time it is ok for the state to interfere with individual's freedom is when?

   A) To protect society
   B) To punish someone
   C) To restrict violent behavior
   D) To teach moral behavior

The correct answer is A:) To protect society.

30) Feminist ethics got its start around what time?

   A) During the 1960's
   B) Just before the 1960's
   C) In the early 1800's
   D) During the time of Aristotle

The correct answer is D:) During the time of Aristotle.

31) Modern approaches to feminist ethics stress which of the following?

   A) Ethic of care over ethic of trust.
   B) Ethic of justice over ethic of trust.
   C) Ethic of care and trust over ethic of justice and rights.
   D) Ethic of justice over ethic of care and trust.

The correct answer is C:) Ethic of care and trust over ethic of justice and rights.

32) In Hinduism, dharma means

   A) The ideas presented in the Bhagavad-Gita
   B) A set of inalienable truths
   C) The ongoing cycle of rebirths
   D) Religion and social duty

The correct answer is D:) Religion and social duty.

Doing Good, Not Doing Harm, Preventing Harm

In our modern age, definitions about what it means to "do good," to "not do harm" and to "prevent harm" all become extremely important because these definitions determine how we will punish people or reward them for certain behaviors. One popular term that is used to determine the definitions of these ideas is known as nonmalficence.

Nonmalficence is generally defined as "not inflicting evil or harm on others." An example of a rule that supports this idea is "do not kill". A more controversial rule of nonmalficence is the rule "do not inflict suffering on others." These rules become especially important in health care ethics. Here, the principle of nonmalficence typically relates to the ongoing debates around both abortion and euthanasia. How we define "harm" plays an integral role in how we define nonmalficence in these cases.

The opposite principle of nonmalficence is the ethical idea of beneficence. Beneficence is what is referred to in the health field as "the doing of good, the prevention of harm and the removal of harm." Some common examples of rules that support beneficence are "you should always protect and defend the rights of others" and "you should rescue a person who is in danger."

In the case of the September 11th attack on the World Trade Center, the ethical preparedness of the New York State Nurses Association was called into question. The nurses association had not been adequately prepared to deal with a disaster of that size. The health care system and many other organizations, at that time, were not prepared to "prevent harm" when a disaster of that size took place on the twin towers. Since that time, however, plans and practices have been put into effect to meet the ethical obligation that these organizations hold for themselves.

Another example of "do not harm" is ahimsa. Ahimsa is usually taken to mean "do no harm," although it is also translated as non-injury, or avoidance of violence. In Hinduism, there is no difference between the soul of an animal and the soul of a human. Therefore, this theory bans eating, hunting, and harming animals and other people in any way. The only exception is the case of self defense, in which case it is accepted. The principle of Ahimsa is also connected with the idea of karma. In other words, doing bad things brings bad consequences, while doing good things brings good consequences.

Obligations to Strangers

The ethical obligations that we have for strangers are largely based on the principle of beneficence. In the modern age, philosophers such as Peter Singer argue that we have an ethical duty to assist people who are suffering from starvation. This is based on the idea of beneficence and Peter Singer has very famously said that "If it is in our power to prevent something very bad happening, without thereby sacrificing anything of comparable moral significance, we ought to do it."

Another modern philosopher, James Rachels, makes the same kind of argument as Singer. He claims that parents have a duty to tend to the necessities of, not only their own children but any child in the world with emergency needs. Rachels says that, as long as it doesn't harm us, then we should adhere to the principle of beneficence concerning other's children as well as our own.

A specific example of this kind of behavior might be where, we already have our primary survival needs satisfied and we are going to enjoy a fancy restaurant dinner which will cost about $60.00. If we hear that a person in another country is close to starving and we know that this money can help them with their emergency needs, it is our ethical obligation to send that money to them.

Special Moral Relationships

The special moral relationship that exists between a parent and their child has become much more significant to lawmakers over the past few decades. It has become obvious that the success of our society strongly depends on this relationship being protected and supported by the society in general. For this reason, the moral specialness of the parent-child relationship has taken on a special legal consideration as well. More and more, the state, local and federal governments are all taking on a deeper involvement in this special moral relationship. This is especially true when a child is being abused or neglected.

By law, this special moral relationship is said to exist anytime a parent either acknowledges themselves to be the parent or when they simply reside with the child. Even in the case where the parent is absent and the state has to intervene, this relationship can be said to continue and the parent can be held legally responsible for things that they don't take care of. In fact, this relationship is so strong that parents or children are actually unable to alter it or destroy it by themselves or even when the two of them agree to end the relationship. This still requires the agreement of the government.

Legally speaking, a parent doesn't just have the right to the custody and the supervision of their child. They have the duty to care for that child and the child has a legal right to receive that care. A parent's duties go beyond simply providing for the daily necessities of life and financial support. A parent must provide for their child's education, health care, social training and must show both love and affection for the child. A parent is even required to discipline the child when it is necessary. In addition to all these legal requirements on the parent, the child also has a legal obligation to yield to their parent's care and to any reasonable form of parental guidance.

In addition to all these rights and duties for the parents and children, the government itself is now said to have legal duties to uphold this special moral relationship between parent and child. The state government, specifically, has the duty to maintain the stability of the family and ensure the proper care of the child. Modern laws now give more power to the government to intervene in cases of child abuse and neglect.

Conflict of Duties

The conflict of duties is one of the biggest problems that philosophers have had to address over the centuries. Immanuel Kant especially ran into problems with this issue because oftentimes two conflicting duties present themselves with equal significance to a person and it is hard to say which one is more important to uphold.

An example of a modern situation might be a case in which you could lie to save someone's life. You would be held to the duty of telling the truth because this is something that is supported by the Categorical Imperative and as a universal maxim and yet you would also be required to preserve a person's life. Which one is more important: truth or human life? In Kantian ethics, the moral action is the one that obeys the **Categorical Imperative** and doesn't violate any of its prohibitions. In this situation it would be impossible to act morally; both lying and telling the truth violate a strict duty. The **Categorical Imperative** are principles that are always valid; they are good in and of themselves; they must be obeyed in all situations and circumstances if our behavior is to observe the moral law.

A modern day example of this situation actually took place with a victim of the Columbine High School killings. When a girl at Columbine was asked about her belief in God she was also told by the killers that, if she answered yes, she would probably be killed. She was then told that, if she answered no, she might be spared. This girl was a Christian and an answer of no would be a lie for her. Her options set up a conflict between her duty to tell the truth and her duty to preserve her own life. She chose to say "yes" and was killed. Kant's discussion about situations like this actually support the choice that this girl made and yet many people are in disagreement with her decision. To uphold the Kantian ideal of strict duties is obviously a very tough decision.

Autonomy and Privacy

In terms of what the law allows in modern society, the right to privacy has been something that has changed over the years. The idea of privacy has slowly become something that must be protected more and more by the government. This privacy also has become the basis for protecting individuals freedom to choose.

Because individuals have the right to privacy, they also have the right to decide whether they want to engage in certain acts. This is their freedom to choose. If someone values their privacy, they may choose not to engage in certain acts and nobody can force them. This personal freedom has developed even further into a "liberty" that is protected by the 14th Amendment. Most importantly, it protects the privacy of the motherhood, marriage, the family, procreation, and child rearing.

The personal autonomy issue for the right of privacy has especially changed in cases dealing with reproductive rights. The Supreme Court firmly established the independent right of privacy in a famous case entitled Griswold vs. Connecticut. In this case, there was a debate over whether the argument of marital privacy could be used to prevent the government from prohibiting the use of contraception between a husband and wife. It was decided that the right to privacy was the more important value in this case and was therefore firmly established by the government. Later, however, another famous case entitled Roe v. Wade said that the governmental could infringe if there was a compelling state interest such as in the case of an unborn child's right to live. The government's interest in stopping an abortion and protecting the safety of the mother outweighed the mother's personal autonomy once the unborn child was viable or could possibly live on its own without her. Before viability, the mother's liberty of personal privacy would prevent the government from interfering.

Fidelity, Accountability and Trustworthiness

In today's modern business world, the character traits of fidelity, accountability and trustworthiness are often weighed out by corporations and public organizations to determine if individual employees will be valuable to the company. This is becoming more and more important as corporations are now watched a lot more carefully than they ever where in the past.

Fidelity is the trait that companies look for where an employee will always have faithfulness to their clients and an allegiance to the public trust. It is the quality of being loyal to an employer or agency and to a profession that makes an employee stand out. In religious organizations, fidelity is considered to be faithfulness to God and this becomes something that goes above and beyond the normal standards of fidelity in business.

Trustworthiness is another trait that is highly valued in the professional world today. When corporations can trust an employee, they can give greater leeway to that employee and don't need to monitor him or her as much. This makes the company more productive and ultimately more successful. Simply refraining from deception is not enough in the case of trustworthiness. Trustworthiness involves many other qualities such as reliability and integrity to one's own word.

Finally, accountability is a quality where a person is always aware of their own actions. An employee who doesn't shift the blame to others or claim credit for other's work is highly valued in today's business world. These employees are in command of what they have and haven't done and they can make an accurate assessment of their actions at any time. They always consider the likely consequences of their behavior and they lead by example.

Veracity

Veracity is a quality or character trait that is often valued in the legal profession and yet it is also highly criticized as well. This is the simple quality of having an adherence to the truth or of being truthful. If a person is said to conform to the facts or the truth with ongoing accuracy or precision, we say that they have veracity. Ralph Waldo Emerson put the character trait of veracity even higher than genius and famously said "The value of genius is in the veracity of its report."

It isn't just people who have veracity. Often times, paperwork or products for sale can be said to have veracity or to be lacking in this quality. In the legal profession, documents and reports are often checked and rechecked for their legal veracity. The notary public who often signs and stamps documents to give them credibility is giving legal veracity to the pertinent legal process that is required in our courts. When products have infringement or patent issues, it is said that their legal veracity may not be in order and the right to sell these items may not be established.

Right to Information

The right to information is a legal issue that often presents itself in both the medical profession and the area of law enforcement. Hospitals often organize a patients "Bill of Rights" that will set forth the rights to information that are given to doctors, nurses, family members and other involved parties in order that good decisions can be made about health care. These issues also involve the right to give informed consent to a certain kind of health treatment and the patient's right to privacy about certain illnesses.

In the area of law enforcement, criminal suspects also have a right to privacy which extends to their right to "not incriminate themselves" before they have a legal trial. They have the right to be represented by a civil attorney and they also have the right to know what they are being accused of and to receive the due process of the law. When an officer arrests a criminal suspect, these rights are read to the suspect because of the principle of law known as the "right to information." This information given is known as the "Miranda warning." It refers to the statement that a police officer must read to suspects when they are taken into custody.

Confidentiality

The International Organization for Standardization or ISO is a modern organization which defines many of the principles and ideas surrounding agreements and contracts between different organizations across different cultures. Confidentiality is a central idea and principle upon which many agreements are based. The ISO defines confidentiality as "the principle that ensures that information is accessible only to those authorized to have access." This is one of the major cornerstones of security in the modern age.

Confidentiality is also significant in terms of modern day ethics when it involves issues around law, medicine, journalism or religion. In legal matters it is often the case that certain communications between professionals and other individuals are considered to be "privileged." They may not be discussed with third parties under the threat of penalty. Lawyers are often required by law to keep confidentiality agreements about anything pertaining to the representation of a client. This serves the purpose of encouraging clients to speak frankly about their cases so that lawyers can carry out a more careful representation. Without the confidentiality agreement, the opposing side in a court case might be able to surprise the lawyer with information that he didn't know about his own client. Lawyers can also hold a fiduciary obligation, a legal obligation to manage and administer assets to the best interest of their client, but not themselves.

In the military branches, confidentiality is often defined in what is classically termed as the "need-to-know" basis. This also forms a cornerstone of security in today's armed forces and in private security firms.

Informed Consent

Informed consent is a condition defined by the law where a person is said to have been given the proper consent by someone else to perform a certain action. In other words, they are "allowed" to perform that action because someone told them they could. A common example of a case like this is in the area of sexual relations. Oftentimes, the communication between two people is not completely clear and informed consent can be hard to determine.

Some examples of problems that arise in determining informed consent are when a person may verbally agree to something from fear or from a misunderstanding about the consequences of their actions. In cases of social pressure, or difficulty with expressing feelings, a person may be unaware of certain facts and they might consent without having given an informed consent. Lawyers often debate the terms of informed consent in the case of rape or sexual abuse cases. Even though a person may think they understand the consequences of an action, they may learn more about a person later on and then deny the validity of the consent they gave. These issues often lead to endless debate amongst lawyers.

Tuskegee Syphilis Experiment

From 1932 through 1972, the U.S. Public Heath Service conducted a clinical study, called the Tuskegee Syphilis Experiment, in Tuskegee, Alabama. Some 399 poor African Americans who were already infected with syphilis were offered free medical exams, burial insurance, and meals to participate in the study. The purpose of the study was to determine the effects of untreated syphilis, so the subjects were never told they had syphilis, or treated for it. Because they didn't give consent, the study is generally considered to have been unethical and now all clinical studies are required to have informed consent from all of their subjects. It is also required that the studies inform the subjects of their diagnoses and accurately report their results.

Although the term medical ethics often refers to doctor patient relations, it can also include issues such as human experimentation, treatment, and informed consent. The idea behind informed consent is that for a patient to consent to a procedure they must understand how it will be done, how it will make them feel, the risks and benefits. This way they are informed about the treatment decisions they are making. Human research, or human experimentation, has many ethical implications. Some general rules for human experimentation include that it is a last resort, the patient has been fully informed and has given their consent, the patient is mentally competent to consent (this excludes mentally disabled people and children), and the treatment is meant to cure the patient.

The **Belmont Report** was written in 1979, in part as a response to the Tuskegee Syphilis Experiment which concluded just a few years prior. The Belmont Report set forth guidelines for human experimentation for the future. It has three main components. They are respect for persons, beneficence, and justice. Respect for persons refers to treating subjects with respect, and honesty. It also includes the principle of informed consent. Beneficence refers to the "do no harm" philosophy. In other words, beneficence is putting the subject at as little risk as possible. The third component, justice, applies to factors such as cost of the study, how the participants are chosen, and equality.

Institutional Responsibilities

In our modern world, there has been a steady increase in lawsuits against teachers over institutional responsibilities. Many legal actions are often started by students, colleagues or people outside the school community. Court cases concerning institutional responsibilities include grading practices, admissions standards, denial of degrees, slander, or personal injury of a faculty member. The increasing lawsuits come from what is thought to be a misuse of appropriate procedures in the institution.

Colleges, universities and other institutions all have a responsibility to ensure that legal representation is given to members of the faculty who undergo a court procedure relating to their professional performance in institutional service.

Professional Code of Ethics

In earlier days, there were really only three professions that were professionally recognized. They were medicine, law and the ministry. These early professions each held their own professional code of ethics such that the members were required to abide by an oath. By taking that oath they were "professing" to abide by a high set of standards and accountability. The code would eliminate any confusion over what was considered to be "ethical" in that profession.

Today, many professional codes have the strength of the law behind them. Some are simply enforced by the professional organization itself with the threat of being fired or losing your membership in the organization if you do not uphold the code. The effectiveness of these professional codes depends on how much the management of an organization supports them by either rewarding or punishing the members.

Paternalism

Paternalism is a term that refers to the way people are governed or treated by an authority. We say that an organization is acting with paternalism when they act in a fatherly manner and provide for people's needs without expecting them to be responsible or to have any particular rights. This is sort of like treating people just as though they were children.

It may seem that the term would imply that the fatherly figure was actually wiser than the people who were being served and that the organization was acting in the best interest of the people. This, however, is not the case with paternalism. The use of this term suggests a more derogatory meaning such that the governing body is thought to be acting in a way that isn't really justified. It places a judgment on organizations and suggests that they are depriving individuals of their personal freedom and not really serving their true interests. Many organizations are often criticized for acting paternally such as governments, corporations and universities but the evidence for these criticisms are always open to debate.

In the case of governments, certain laws that force citizens to follow particular rules and are supposedly "for their own safety" will often be considered paternalistic. The seat belt law has been popularly criticized as being paternalistic. Many people have often felt that they were more than capable of looking after themselves in terms of their own seat belt usage and that the government should not intervene in this area. For this reason, there is often a negative stigma attached to the word "paternalism" when it is used in this context.

Another very famous example of paternalistic legislation came during the time of Prohibition in the United States. Alcohol was changed to an illegal substance and this was said to be a form of paternalistic legislation on the part of the government.

Retributive and Distributive Justice

Retributive justice is the theory that punishments are justified because criminals create an imbalance in the order of society which has to be taken care of by action. This often means harsh punishment and supporters of this theory often use the phrase "an eye for an eye, a tooth for a tooth." This theory was made very popular in the early 1980's when the law community began to feel as though there had been many practical failings of the law in previous decades.

Distributive justice, however, has to do with a strict or radical form of equality that is said to be necessary for all people. This theory was made popular by the philosopher John Rawls who argued against Utilitarianism and more in terms of a welfare based principle of justice. Rawls believes that we have an obligation to give more to the underprivileged people and less to the privileged.

Ronald Dworkin

Ronald Dworkin was an admired legal philosopher of the 20th century. Dworkin was born in 1931 in Rhode Island, and went on to amaze professors at both Harvard and Oxford. His theories have been given the title of legal interpretivism. Dworkin rejected the traditions views of the objectivity of law, and instead claimed that they law was open to interpretation.

Not only was law to be interpreted, according to Dworkin, but it possesses a morality in itself. Legal interpretivism argues that any situation that calls upon the law requires some collection of both moral and legal principles to be understood. The two combined in relation to a given situation result in an interpretation of law that defines legal and moral precedent. Dworkin was also concerned with the concept of equality. He argued that individual talents do not create grounds for inequality, and felt that equality and liberty do not have to stand in opposition to each other. According to Dworkin, liberty inherently requires that all have equal rights to act freely. Therefore, where inequality exists, liberty suffers.

Balancing Harms

The idea of balancing harms in ethics is best understood in terms of examples. The case of euthanasia is a common area where the idea of balancing harms comes into play. When a person intentionally takes someone's life, this is often defined as harmful and can be categorized as murder. This is especially true if the motive for doing this were simply to collect an inheritance. However, when the motive is to relieve the pain of someone who is suffering in the hospital from a terminal illness, killing suddenly seems like a more humane act and one that could be defined as compassionate. In a case like this, the idea of balancing harms comes into play.

On the one side, a person could decide to go ahead and impose pain on the hospital victim by forcing them to endure a long, slow death. On the other side, they could allow for a system where society considered it just to terminate a person's life in special circumstances. Finding the correct way to determine these special circumstances without exposing people to criminal charges involves balancing the harms that exist in both sides of the example.

Ethics and Environmental Ties

Aldo Leopold was a farmer who lived from 1887-1948. He wrote *The Sand County Almanac* which was published in 1949. In the book, he set forth his idea of the "land ethic," also known as the Theory of Moral Land. Leopold saw the "land" as a "community" which included animals, soil, and people, instead of seeing people as masters of the land. The basic principle of the land ethic was that humans are a part of the environment. Humans should be taking care of it, not abusing it.

The Native American philosophy is much more in tune with nature than that of European cultures. Native Americans view the land as more of a consciousness than the scientific view of rocks, animals and elements. For example, when Europeans were settling the American continent, many Native Americans could not understand how the Europeans felt they could "claim" the land. To them, it was independent of human activities, and wasn't something a person could own. Many believed the earth and nature to have mysterious powers. Their Shamans were people with the ability to contact the spirit world.

The idea behind sustainability is long term maintenance and endurance. Some people view the current state of the world as unethical. The exploitation of natural resources cause problems because the current demand is great enough that the environment cannot sustain it. For example, it is widely accepted that the earth's oil supply is finite. This means that when it's gone, it's gone. This is a resource that cannot be sustained, especially as demand continues to increase. Another example is with trees. As demand for trees increases, their abundance decreases. It's possible to hit a point where there aren't enough trees left to fulfill the demand, because they are cut down faster than they grow. These are some reasons that many people find it unethical to exploit natural resources and push for sustainable lifestyles.

Environmental Racism

Environmental racism is essentially any practice which harms an environment that is low income, or where a specific race (often minority) is prevalent, more than it does other environments. For example, if a new school is built in an area with high socioeconomic status, and not in an area with a low socioeconomic status that would be an example of environmental racism. Another common example is if landfills are placed closer to African American or Latino communities than they are to communities which are predominantly white.

Sample Test Questions
Section 2: Ethical Analysis

Questions 32-37 are based on the following situation.

Mrs. Jones is a nurse who works in the local hospital. She is a single mother with three children and she supports them all financially because her husband is gone. At the hospital, one of Mrs. Jones patients has been diagnosed with a terminal illness and is suffering a lot of pain each day. The doctors have told her that this patient will not survive another month. Although the doctors have prescribed a pain medication for this patient, the rules of the hospital state that a patient can only receive this medication every four hours. Although there is an excess of this kind of medication at the hospital, the patient still begins to experience extreme pain after only two hours of receiving the medication and begins yelling out in pain after three hours. It is very easy for Mrs. Jones to administer the medication every three hours but she could also get fired if she were caught doing this.

With only the information provided in this passage, is the following an issue that could contribute to maleficence on the part of Mrs. Jones?

32) Putting her job and salary at risk in order to relieve the suffering of her patient.

33) Asking the head physician to increase the dosage for the patient.

34) Administering the medication early when nobody else is around to see her actions.

Is the following an appropriate course of action for Mrs. Jones to follow concerning the principle of beneficence?

35) Convince the doctor to increase the dosage of the patient.

36) Sit with the patient, listen to their complaints and empathize with their pain.

37) Work overtime to save more money and send her children to college.

Question 38-41 are short essay questions based on the following situation.

Mr. Smith is a successful businessman who drives through an impoverished section of the city on his way to work each day. He often sees children begging for change as he stops at a stoplight. Mr. Smith has heard that many of these children work for larger syndicates and that these syndicates are run by abusive adults. The adults keep the children on the streets to make money for themselves. They are often addicted to drugs or simply abusing the children for their own selfish needs. Mr. Smith does not know which children work for these syndicates and which do not. He is hesitant to give money to the children and cannot decide what to do.

Write one or two paragraphs for each question.

38) What are the most significant moral principles or issues that would have a bearing on Mr. Smiths decision and why?

39) Which ethical position, Consequentialist or Deontological, do you see as the best in this situation and how does it support the decision you think Mr. Smiths should make?

40) Describe the opposite view to your position in the most reasonable way that you can, and make the best ethical arguments you can for this opposing view.

41) Reconsider your original position in question 39 and explain how you would address the opposing argument you made in question 40.

Questions 42-45 are based on the following situation.

Sarah is an 18 year old girl who is graduating from high school this year and making a decision about where to go to school next year. She is an excellent singer and has won several singing contests in her town. There is a music college nearby but she lives in an impoverished country where there are almost no jobs available in music. When she graduates from Music College, she would have to move out of her country to the United States. The United States is only issuing foreign VISAS to either teachers or nurses but not to musicians. Sarah will have to study nursing first before she can get to the U.S.

Write one paragraph on how each of the following issues relate to certain ethical principles of justice for Sarah?

42) Sarah's nature and natural desire is to sing and she does not feel any inclination to be a nurse.

43) Over half of the graduates from music colleges in the U.S. go on to find jobs in their field but none of them find jobs in Sarah's country.

44) By completing her nursing degree and emigrating to the U.S., Sarah can eventually continue with her music and become a successful singer.

45) While working on her nursing degree, Sarah discovers that she has an inborn desire to help people and to care for them. She is no longer concerned about emigrating to the U.S. or about the laws concerning her VISA. She would rather pursue nursing in her own country.

Questions 46-52 are based on the following situation.

Janet is 10 years old and was born into a family of 7 children. Her father moved away to another country when she was three and has not been heard of since. In order to help out, Janet's aunt agreed to take care of her and to send her to school. Janet only sees her real mother in the summertime and on holidays.

Is the following an issue that could contribute to negligence for Janet's mother?

46) Janet's mother yells at her when she is bad.

47) Janet's mother believes in always allowing her children to do as they please.

48) Janet's aunt secretly keeps her out of school.

Is the following an appropriate course of action for the government in relation to Janet?

49) Allowing Janet the freedom to decide where she will live.

50) Investigating into allegations that Janet is being neglected.

51) Holding Janet's mother legally responsible when her aunt doesn't send her to school.

52) Holding Janet's father financially responsible for her.

Questions 53-56 are based on the following situation.

Mr. Jones is a magazine publisher who has been to court many times in his life for publishing photographs and materials which have been considered immoral. Mr. Jones' lawyers would often argue that the right to publish these materials was based on the First Amendment of the Constitution which states that "Congress shall make no law respecting an establishment of religion, or prohibiting the free exercise thereof; or abridging the freedom of speech, or of the press; or the right of the people peaceably to assemble, and to petition the Government for a redress of grievances."

Write one paragraph on how each of the following issues relate to certain ethical principles of natural law for Mr. Jones?

53) Mr. Jones' lawyers argue that the photographs in his magazines simply illustrate the way people "naturally are."

54) Mr. Jones' lawyers argue that repressing your natural human desires only leads to other psychological problems in your life.

55) Mr. Jones' lawyers argue that his photographs never interfere with a person's ability to work or support themselves and, in some cases even help people to find jobs.

56) The opposing prosecution against Mr. Jones argues that Mr. Jones' photographs are "corrupting the youth."

Questions 57-60 are based on the following situation.

A famous philosopher and mathematician named Blaise Pascal invented a famous philosophical argument known as "Pascal's Wager." It describes the logical reason why every person should choose to act morally. Pascal argues that there are only four options available in life. Option 1 is when a person acts immorally in their life and discovers after they die that there is a Heaven and a Hell. This person would be deeply disappointed. Option 2 involves a person who acts immorally but finds that there really is no life after death and therefore no punishment. This person may be considered to be mildly happy. Option 3 involves a person acting morally all their life and also discovering that there was no reward or punishment after they died. This person would also be considered to be only mildly happy. Option 4 involves a person who acted morally all their lives and found that there was a Heaven and a Hell after they died. This person would be considered to be extremely happy. Pascal argues that the simple logic of a "wager" would make it obvious to anyone that they should choose to act morally. With a 50% chance of eternal salvation or damnation, it only makes simple sense to place your money on morality and the chance for eternal salvation. Eternal damnation is simply too much of a risk.

Write one or two paragraphs for each question.

57) How could Pascal's reasoning be applied to the Kantian dilemma that the student at Columbine High School was faced with?

58) If Thomas Aquinas was placing his bets on Pascal's wager, how would he choose to act during his life, according to which specific law or laws?

59) If Immanuel Kant was placing his bets on Pascal's wager, how would he choose to act during his life, according to which specific law or laws?

60) How would you argue that Pascal's wager is not enough to get a person to Heaven? What other things might be necessary according to the view of other philosophers?

Questions 61-67 are based on the following situation.

A large corporation is planning to hire 300 new employees and train them to be managers at their local stores throughout the Southern States of the U.S. In order to decide which applicants will receive job offers, the company has designed a questionnaire to help determine which applicants are more qualified for the job of manager. They have also made a formal statement about their policies and values to the prospective employees.

Is the following a character trait in an employee that would be valuable to a managerial position? Briefly explain your answer.

61) The applicant states that they usually choose one place or one product that they like and they stick with that choice for a long time.

62) The applicant states that they are in favor of paternalism in corporate governing.

63) The applicant states that they do see weaknesses in their own behavior and they admit to this fact when an authority questions them.

Is the following a quality of a corporation that would be attractive for a prospective employee? Briefly explain your answer.

64) The legal representatives for the corporation are known for their veracity.

65) The corporation has a strict code of ethics that is clearly outlined and must be signed before hiring.

66) Institutional responsibilities are something that the company places on its individual employees.

67) The company is very paternalistic in its policy toward employees.

Questions 68-73 are based on the following situation.

Jane is five months pregnant and wants to obtain a legal abortion. Simple abortions without a court case are only legal up until three months pregnancy. Her claim is based on the fact that she did not give informed consent to the father of her baby. In court, her lawyers will argue that John, the biological father, did not tell her that he was married and Jane only discovered this fact after she became pregnant.

Is the following a positive aspect of Jane's case? Explain your answer in terms of "informed consent."

68) Jane agreed to a relationship with John only because she thought he was unmarried.

69) After five months of pregnancy, abortion is only legal in the case of rape or serious health risks to the mother.

70) Jane never asked John if he was married until after she was pregnant.

Is the following a positive aspect of John's case?

71) John was afraid to tell Jane about his marriage because he loves her and didn't want her to reject him.

72) Jane often spoke with John about an affair she had been through with another married man.

73) Jane found out about John's marriage just after her eighth week of pregnancy.

Questions 74-77 are based on the following situation.

A certain political group meets every Friday to discuss their community projects and their strategy for changing the present laws in their town. This group believes that everybody should receive equal pay for their jobs regardless of what they choose for a career and they also feel that their should be strict laws that punish employers who do not distribute their wealth equally to all employees. The group also believes in retributive justice for both employers and employees.

Write one paragraph on each question.

74) What kind of penalties should the group impose on companies in terms of retributive justice for unequal distribution of pay?

75) What argument would John Rawls use to justify the groups policy for distributive justice?

76) If an employee were to damage the property of the company, what type of consequences would this political group impose on the employee?

77) What problems would likely emerge in a company that instituted distributive justice into their payroll system?

Questions 78-81 are based on the following situation.

Mrs. Smith has always valued a great meal that is prepared with the finest quality of tastes and decorations. Her husband, however, prefers a restaurant that serves an "all you can eat" buffet so that he can really get the most food for his money. The two of them often argue over which restaurant to visit but their daughter often tells them that their arguing only originates from inside their mind and any restaurant is just fine for her.

Answer each question and write one paragraph explaining your answer.

78) Which philosopher would likely agree with Mrs. Smith about the type of restaurant to visit?

79) Which philosopher would likely agree with Mr. Smith about the type of restaurant to visit?

80) Which philosopher would likely agree with the Smith's daughter about the type of restaurant to visit?

81) Based on the answer you gave in question 82, can you describe a restaurant that might be more attractive to the Smith's daughter?

Questions 82-89 are based on the following situation.

A large corporation is being accused of paternalistic tendencies. They want to avoid this criticism so they are examining their policies and trying to decide what to change about their company.

Are the following facts a concern for this company and something that they might change in order to avoid criticism? Briefly explain your answer.

82) The company offers the option for employees to purchase the company stock at a reduced price.

83) The company offers promotion incentives to single women with no children.

84) The company favors equal opportunity employment.

85) Secretary positions are not eligible for promotion within the company.

86) The company offers paid vacation to anyone with over two years employment.

Would the following changes result in a genuine solution to the problem of paternalism in this company? Briefly explain your answer.

87) The company decides to keep their hiring and promotion statistics confidential in the future.

88) The company decides to offer a paid leave of absence to female employees who become pregnant after one year of working for the company.

89) The company announces a new policy of firing any employee who speaks negatively to the press about the workings of the company.

Questions 90-93 are based on the following situation.

Susan is 21 years old and recently became pregnant. Her boyfriend has left her and she does not have the money to support a child on her own. She is one year away from receiving her college degree and does not want to tell her parents about her pregnancy. She would like to receive an abortion at the clinic where her mother works as a receptionist.

Is the following an ethical concern that which would exist for the doctor performing the abortion on Susan? Briefly explain your answer.

90) The doctor is close friends with Susan.

91) Susan has specifically requested that the doctor not tell her mother about the pregnancy.

92) Susan's mother is a Christian and believes that abortion is a sin.

93) Susan's health could be jeopardized by having an abortion.

Questions 94-100 are based on the following situation

A plane carrying seven passengers has been hijacked by terrorists who are holding one of the passengers at gunpoint. The passenger is a prominent politician whose philosophical beliefs are not known. The terrorists have strapped a bomb to the politician's waist and have demanded that he release classified information.

What concerns would the politician have if he was a Kantian in each of the following situations? Explain your answer in one paragraph.

94) If the politician lies to the terrorists, he knows he can persuade them to disengage the bomb.

95) The politician knows that the classified information will not be life threatening if released.

96) The plane is carrying an atomic bomb that could detonate over a major population area.

What concerns would the politician have if he was a Utilitarian in each of the following situations? Explain your answer in one paragraph.

97) The passengers have all insisted that the politician maintain the classified nature of the information being demanded by the terrorists.

98) If revealed, the classified information would not be life threatening to anyone but would cost billions of dollars to the government.

99) If revealed, the classified information would create a health pandemic that would not be fatal but would cause illness in thousands of people for years to come.

100) It is absolutely impossible to determine any of the consequences that will result from the politician's decision.

Answers to Sample Test Questions (32-100)

32) YES
33) NO
34) NO
35) YES
36) YES
37) YES
38) The morality of the action itself vs. the consequences of the action, duties to strangers, justice as fairness based on veil of ignorance.
39) Consequentialist only supports giving in certain situations but Deontological supports giving for its own sake.
40) Consequentialist ethics is weak if you can't determine the consequences, Deontological is weak if the results of the action are harmful and shown to be necessarily connected.
41) For Deontological argument, disprove the necessary connection between action and consequence. For Consequentialist argument prove the necessity of the connection.
42) Plato's Theory of Justice prescribes a society where people can follow their nature.
43) Rawls Theory of Justice uses the liberty principle to state that nobody should have freedom until others have freedom; difference principle says the poor and disadvantaged should get special treatment.
44) Rawls Theory of Procedural Justice or any of the utilitarian theories of ethics which focus on outcomes are justified and shown to be successful based on the outcome in this example.
45) Feminist ethics of care is discovered to be true in this case.
46) NO
47) YES
48) YES
49) NO
50) YES
51) YES

52) YES

53) Aquinas argues for the pursuit of our natural inclinations inclusive of reproduction.

54) Aquinas also argues for a pursuit of reason which would dictate that repression of reproductive inclination would result in psychological problems.

55) Aquinas argues for the natural inclination of self-preservation or to support ourselves.

56) The argument depends upon the nature of the photographs and whether they express natural inclinations, the lawyer's argument also resembles the charge against Socrates of "corrupting the youth."

57) Choosing to tell the truth about a belief in God is correct under the Kantian ethics and is compatible with Pascal's wager.

58) Aquinas advocates learning about and following natural law as it is given by Divine Providence and will bring you to Heaven.

59) Kant would advocate following the Categorical Imperative in all cases.

60) Besides just choosing to act morally, one may need to learn what constitutes a moral act. This is different in Greek, Biblical, Consequentialist, Deontological, Feminist ethics and others.

61) Yes...Fidelity.

62) No...Paternalism is a derogatory term about governance.

63) Yes...Accountability.

64) Yes...Veracity is the adherence to truth.

65) Yes...A clear code means clear expectations on the employee and less confusion.

66) No...Institutional responsibilities should belong to the company.

67) No...Paternalism does not support the best interests of employees.

68) Yes...Jane was not properly informed about her partner and therefore was incapable of giving informed consent to him.

69) Yes...Informed consent may determine the definition of rape, in which case Jane may attempt to charge her partner with rape and this may not be a detrimental aspect of her case.

70) No...The lack of informed consent may be partly the responsibility of Jane based on the fact that she never asked John about his past.

71) Yes...Lawyers may garner sympathy for John based on his love for Jane.

72) Yes...Lack of informed consent may be attributed to Jane as she has a history of this behavior.

73) Yes...Jane had four weeks to obtain a legal abortion without a trial but did not take advantage of this opportunity.

74) Retributive justice demands "an eye for an eye" so presumably the company would pay a financial penalty equal to the lowered pay they gave out to employees.

75) Rawls argues that special treatment should only be given to the poor or disadvantaged.

76) The employee would have to pay for the cost of the damaged property or replace it.

77) Employees would lose the motivation to improve because the incentives for pay raise and promotion would be gone.

78) Mill

79) Bentham

80) Epicurus

81) A tranquil environment

82) No concern

83) Yes concern...staying single and without children may not be in the best interests of certain women

84) No concern

85) Yes concern...This may be a paternalistic bias toward secretaries

86) No concern

87) Not a genuine solution but only covering up the problem

88) Genuine solution to the problem in 83

89) Not a genuine solution but only covering up the problem

90) Not an ethical concern

91) Ethical concern of right to privacy

92) Not an ethical concern of the doctor

93) Ethical concern of "avoiding or preventing harm"

94) Conflict of duties between telling the truth and preserving life

95) Conflict of duties between confidentiality and preserving life

96) Conflict of duties between confidentiality and preserving life

97) Happiness of passengers vs. happiness of others

98) Happiness derived from finances of the government vs. happiness of maintaining confidential information

99) Happiness derived from health of millions vs. happiness of maintaining classified information

100) This is the primary argument against Utilitarianism and which makes it impossible to determine practical moral behavior he ancestral spirits must be honored. Often this is considered "ancestor worship."

Additional Sample Test Questions

1) Which of the following statements is correct?

   A) In Hinduism there is no difference between the souls of animals and humans, so it is wrong to harm either in any way.
   B) Ahimsa literally means "do no harm" and is a central idea of Hinduism.
   C) Ahimsa supports a person's actions in self defense.
   D) All of the above are true.

The correct answer is D:) All of the above are true. Answers A, B, and C are all correct statements about Ahimsa and its application in Hinduism.

2) Which of the following were talked about in Jesus's Sermon on the Mount?

   A) Attitude, oaths, and forgiveness
   B) Prayer, judgment, and false prophets
   C) Murder, adultery and marriage
   D) All of the above

The correct answer is D:) All of the above. The Sermon on the Mount can be considered a summary of Christian ethics. In it, Christ essentially addresses the Ten Commandments.

3) Which of the following is now required of clinical studies?

   A) Informed consent
   B) Communication of diagnoses
   C) Accurate reporting of test results
   D) All of the above

The correct answer is D:) All of the above.

4) Which of the following is true of the Tuskegee Syphilis Experiment?

   A) It took place from 1832 through 1872.
   B) The ethics of the study have been questioned because they never told the subjects that they had syphilis or treated them for it.
   C) 3,000 African Americans were part of the study.
   D) The study was completely ethical because they didn't negatively affect the subjects in any way.

The correct answer is B:) The ethics of the study were questionable because they never told the subjects that they had syphilis or treated them for it. The study took place in 1932-1972, and included 399 subjects.

5) Which of the following is NOT an example of environmental racism?

   A) Building a new school in an area with a higher socioeconomic area, instead of a lower one.
   B) The popularity of the practice of slavery in colonial and early American history.
   C) Placing a landfill closer to an area which is predominantly African American than to an area which is predominantly white.
   D) All of the above are examples of environmental racism.

The correct answer is B:) The popularity of the practice of slavery in colonial and early American history. Although the practice of slavery does pertain to racism, it is not an example of environmental racism.

6) Which of the following is NOT a rule for human research?

   A) The patient is fully informed and has given consent.
   B) The patient is mentally competent to consent.
   C) The treatment is relatively fast acting.
   D) The treatment is meant to cure the patient.

The correct answer is C:) The treatment is relatively fast acting. Answers A, B, and D are all requirements that must be met before human experimentation occurs.

7) Which of the following was not a principle of Leopold's land ethic?

   A) People are rulers of the earth and since it is in their care, they should take care of it.
   B) The land is a community, not an object to be controlled by men.
   C) It is the responsibility of mankind to take care of the land.
   D) Humans are a part of the environment.

The correct answer is A:) People rulers of the earth and since it is in their care, they should take care of it. Leopold's land ethic stated that people were a part of the environment, and that's why they should take care of it.

8) Which of the following describes the principle of Ahimsa?

   A) Literally "do no harm" the principle of Ahimsa bans the harming of humans or animals.
   B) Ahimsa does not support violence of any kind, including that in self defense.
   C) Ahimsa openly supports violence, especially in the case of self defense.
   D) Ahimsa works in direct contrast with the theory of karma. Instead it believes that there are no actual consequences for a person's actions.

The correct answer is A:) Literally "do no harm" the principle of Ahimsa bans the harming of human or animals. Answers B is nearly correct, except in the second half. Ahimsa does not support violence of any kind, however it does allow for self defense.

9) In what book did Leopold set forth the idea of the land ethic?

   A) Aldo Leopold: Land Ethics
   B) Round River
   C) The Sand County Almanac
   D) Game Management

The correct answer is C:) The Sand County Almanac. This book was written by Aldo Leopold, however it was not published until a year after his death.

10) Which of the following is NOT a main component of the Belmont Report?

   A) Respect for persons
   B) Beneficence
   C) Justice
   D) Honesty

The correct answer is D:) Honesty. Respect for persons is the first component of the Belmont Report, and it includes honesty. However, honesty alone is not a main component of the Belmont Report.

11) Which of the following is an example of active euthanasia?

   A) Disconnecting the life support machine from a person who still has brain function.
   B) Refusing to perform a potentially life saving surgery.
   C) Legally taking a person in a coma off of life support.
   D) Knowingly administering a lethal overdose of prescribed medication.

The correct answer is D:) Knowingly administering a lethal overdose of prescribed medication. In active euthanasia, a person actively brings about a patients death. Answers A, B, and C are all examples of passive euthanasia.

12) Which of the following is NOT true?

   A) Reason and rationality were two main components of the Enlightenment.
   B) The purpose of the Enlightenment was to combat ignorance and superstition.
   C) One Enlightenment thinker was Immanuel Kant.
   D) Supporters of Enlightenment worked to support Catholic beliefs using science.

The correct answer is D:) Supporters of the Enlightenment worked to support Catholic beliefs using science. On the contrary the Enlightenment thinkers worked to combat the superstition and power of the Catholic church.

13) Which philosopher believed that suicide was acceptable only when serving a bigger purpose?

A) Sir Francis Bacon
B) John Dewey
C) John Locke
D) Aristotle

The correct answer is C:) John Locke. In most aspects Locke believed that a person was not justified in committing suicide.

14) Why did Locke believe that suicide was unethical?

A) Locke did not believe that suicide was unethical. On the contrary, he believed that every person had the right to determine how and when their life would end.
B) He believed suicide is a form of murder and it should be legally and ethically just as wrong.
C) Because it is unfair to all the other people that the person knows.
D) He believed that human beings belong to God, making it His decision how long they live.

The correct answer is D:) He believed that human beings belong to God, making it His decision how long they live. Locke believed that suicide was not justified because it was not a person's right.

15) Which of the following is does NOT relate to medical ethics?

A) Doctor patient relations
B) Informed consent
C) Human experimentation
D) Where the patient lives

The correct answer is D:) Where the patient lives. Doctor patient relations, informed consent, and human experimentation are all issues which relate to medical ethics.

16) How does the Native American philosophy compare to European philosophy of nature?

   A) Native American philosophy is much more in tune with nature.
   B) European philosophy is much more in tune with nature.
   C) Neither philosophy is in tune with nature at all.
   D) There is no difference between the two philosophies. Both are equally in tune with nature.

The correct answer is A:) Native American philosophy is much more in tune with nature. Native Americans view the world as more independent of human action then do other cultures.

17) Which of the following is NOT considered euthanasia?

   A) Taking a brain dead person, whose heart and lungs are still functioning, off of life support.
   B) Knowingly administering a lethal overdose of a prescribed medication to a patient.
   C) Do not resuscitate orders.
   D) Taking a person in a coma off of life support.

The correct answer is A:) Taking a brain dead person, whose heart and lungs are still functioning, off of life support. If a person has been pronounced brain dead, they are no longer considered living, so it would not be euthanasia. On the other hand, people in a coma are considered alive.

18) Which of the following correctly describes a way in which pacifism applies to ethics?

   A) Companies which sell pacifiers are often unethical in their treatment of employees.
   B) It is unethical for groups which are opposed to the government to protest war.
   C) Pacifism has no actual or accepted application to ethics.
   D) Many people question whether it is unethical to force a pacifist to fight in a war.

The correct answer is D:) Many people question whether it is unethical to force a pacifist to fight in a war.

19) Which of the following is NOT true of Native American philosophy?

A) Shamans were people with the ability to contact the spirit world.
B) The earth and nature were believed to have mysterious powers.
C) Native Americans were upset when Europeans began settling because they considered the land to be theirs.
D) Native American philosophy promotes respect for nature.

The correct answer is C:) Native Americans were upset when Europeans began settling because they considered the land to be theirs. Ownership of land was not a Native American philosophy. They didn't believe that a person could own the earth.

20) A doctor allows a patient suffering from a painful terminal illness to take a lethal dose of their medication to alleviate their suffering. This is an example of

A) Speciesism
B) Neglect
C) Euthanasia
D) Manslaughter

The correct answer is C:) Euthanasia. Euthanasia is often referred to as physician assisted suicide. The ethical merits of such actions are deeply contested and are a popular topic of ethical debate.

21) Who were Cain and Abel?

A) The first two prophets
B) The children of Adam and Eve
C) The last two prophets in the Old Testament
D) The last two prophets in the New Testament

The correct answer is B:) The children of Adam and Eve.

22) Which of the following would be considered a sustainable practice?

A) Use of fossil fuels
B) Cutting down trees
C) Recycling
D) Excessive hunting

The correct answer is C:) Recycling. Use of fossil fuels, cutting down trees, and excessive hunting are all examples of exploitative activities which harm the environment.

23) Which of the following can NOT be learned from the story of Cain and Abel?

   A) It is possible to get away with doing things which are wrong.
   B) Negative consequences come from a person not doing what they're told.
   C) It is not possible for a person to hide their sins.
   D) Jealousy and greed motivate people to do good things.

The correct answer is A:) It is possible to get away with doing things which are wrong. On the contrary, Cain could not hide his sin from the Lord, and was punished.

24) What are stem cells?

   A) Cells which are taken from the stem of a plant for research about plant development.
   B) Cells which have the potential to become any type of cell.
   C) Cells which are taken from a plant's stem in order to learn more about plant structure.
   D) Human cells taken from the brain stem.

The correct answer is B:) Cells which have the potential to become any type of cell.

25) Which of the following is NOT an event in the book of Exodus?

   A) Moses sets forth the Ten Commandments.
   B) Cain kills his brother Abel, becoming the world's first murderer.
   C) The Israelites are led out of bondage in Egypt.
   D) The Israelites covenant with the Lord.

The correct answer is B:) Cain kills his brother Abel, becoming the world's first murderer. This happens in Genesis, while all the other three answers all happen in Exodus.

26) What matters did the Law of Moses concern?

   I. Political
   II. Religious
   III. Moral

   A) Only II
   B) I and II only
   C) II and III only
   D) I, II, and III

The correct answer is D:) I, II, and III. The Law of Moses directed the Israelites in essentially every aspect of their lives.

27) Which of the following is NOT true of The Sermon on the Mount?

   A) It can be considered a summary of Christian ethical beliefs.
   B) The Sermon on the Mount was a sermon given to Jesus, recorded in Matthew chapters 5-7.
   C) Topics of the Sermon on the Mount include forgiveness, adultery, murder, false prophets, and more.
   D) Christ essentially discusses the Ten Commandments.

The correct answer is B:) The Sermon on the Mount was a sermon given to Jesus, recorded in Matthew chapter 5-7. Answer B is the opposite of correct. The sermon was given "by" Jesus, not "to" him.

28) Which of the following are NOT included in the Law of Moses?

   A) Ten Commandments
   B) Laws of business dealing and politics
   C) Laws concerning morality and physical purity
   D) A description of the physical laws of the world

The correct answer is D:) A description of the physical laws of the world. The Law of Moses was highly detailed, and discussed business, politics, morality and physical purity. It also included the Ten Commandments.

29) What law is associated with the Old Testament?

   A) The Law of God
   B) The Fifteen Commandments
   C) The Law of Moses
   D) The Ten Commandments

The correct answer is C:) The Law of Moses. The law was given to the Israelites after being led out of bondage by Moses. Although the Ten Commandments are associated with the Old Testament, the Law of Moses is the correct answer because the Ten Commandments are a part of the Law of Moses.

30) Which component of the Belmont Report does the "do no harm" philosophy apply to?

   A) Respect for persons
   B) Beneficence
   C) Justice
   D) None of the above

The correct answer is B:) Beneficence. Beneficence refers to putting the subject at as little risk as possible, while still conducting research. In other words "do no harm."

31) What ethical conflict pertains to the Law of Retaliation?

   A) There is no ethical conflict related to the Law of Retaliation.
   B) The Law of Retaliation is too merciful to be a basis for ethical principles.
   C) All people are essentially the same, and God expects the same purity of all.
   D) The struggle between being just and being merciful.

The correct answer is D:) The struggle between being just and being merciful. The Law of Retaliation is completely just, but allows no place for mercy.

32) Which of the following BEST describes beneficence?

   A) Actions taken to increase the general happiness of oneself
   B) Actions taken to injure others
   C) Actions taken to prevent harm to others
   D) Actions taken to benefit others

The correct answer is D:) Actions taken to benefit others. The objective of beneficent actions is to benefit others. This goes beyond simply removing harm. For example, doctors are expected to help patients improve, not to simply remove harmful symptoms.

33) Social custom regarded as moral and religious duty?

   A) Karma
   B) Justice
   C) Dharma
   D) All of the above

The correct answer is C:) Dharma.

34) What is political freedom?

   A) A person's right to take part in public affairs.
   B) Political freedom is the right to vote.
   C) Political freedom is the specific term for freedom of speech.
   D) None of the above are correct descriptions of political freedom.

The correct answer is A:) A person's right to take part in public affairs. Answers B and C both give examples of freedoms included in political freedom, however only Answer A actually describes it.

35) Which of the following does NOT describe the Law of Retaliation?

   A) An eye for an eye
   B) Complete mercy
   C) Punishment equal to crime
   D) Complete justice

The correct answer is B:) Complete mercy. It is actually the opposite. The Law of Retaliation is characterized by complete justice, because the punishment is equal to the crime.

36) Which of the following correctly describes the difference between Thrasymachus and Thucydides?

A) Thrasymachus lived in 500 BC and Thucydides lived in 800 BC.
B) Thucydides believed that justice was the struggle between powers, whereas Thrasymachus believed power struggles to be a danger to justice.
C) Thrasymachus believed that justice was the struggle between powers, whereas Thucydides believed power struggles to be a danger to justice.
D) Thrasymachus and Thucydides had identical belief systems.

The correct answer is C:) Thrasymachus believed that justice was the struggle between powers, whereas Thucydides believed power struggles to be a danger to justice. Thucydides said, "Right, as the world goes, is only in question between equals in power, while the strong do what they can and the weak suffer what they must."

37) Which of the following philosopher's was known for their belief that "might makes right"?

A) Galileo
B) Aristotle
C) John Calvin
D) Thrasymachus

The correct answer is D:) Thrasymachus.

38) The belief that a person's actions and their ethical consequences will effect their next life refers to what?

A) Dharma
B) Generosity
C) Karma
D) Relationships

The correct answer is C:) Karma.

39) What is the basic idea behind sustainability?

   A) The ability of a person to hold their breath for a really long time to conserve oxygen.
   B) Long term maintenance of the environment and endurance of the human race.
   C) Being vegetarian because current rates of consumption of meat do not allow animal populations adequate time to sustain themselves.
   D) It's acceptable to exploit natural resources because humans are the conquerors of the world.

The correct answer is B:) Long term maintenance of the environment and endurance of the human race. Answer C is a specific example of a sustainable practice, but it does not describe the main idea. Answer D explains essentially the exact opposite.

40) Which of the following is an example of affirmative action?

   A) If someone acts based on a principle that they agree with.
   B) When a person votes for a person whose viewpoints they agree with.
   C) A person protesting against a product which they don't agree with.
   D) A university offering more scholarship opportunities to applicants from minority races.

The correct answer is D:) A university offering more scholarship opportunities to applicants from minority races. Affirmative action attempts to benefit underrepresented groups based on race, gender or religion.

41) What does Rita Manning believe?

   A) Generosity is the main component involved in how ethical a person is.
   B) There is no real difference between ethics of care and ethics of justice.
   C) Relationships affect people the least when they are discussing ethics.
   D) The most important aspect affecting a person's perception of ethics is relationships.

The correct answer is D:) The most important aspect affecting a person's perception of ethics is relationships. Rita Manning is a strong supporter of the ethics of care.

42) What is affirmative action?

   A) When a person actively affirms that they belong to a specific religion.
   B) A term which applies only to feminism and helping underrepresented women.
   C) A philosophy which attempts to benefit underrepresented groups based on race, gender or religion.
   D) A famous law firm in Dallas, Texas which actively seeks out racism cases.

The correct answer is C:) A philosophy which attempts to benefit underrepresented groups based on race, gender or religion. While it could in cases apply to feminism (Answer B), affirmative action is a general term best explained by Answer C.

43) What is environmental racism?

   A) Any practice which harms an environment that is low income or racially homogenous more than it does other environments.
   B) Discriminating against certain types of plants. For example, some people refuse to plant rose bushes.
   C) A theory which revolves around a philosophy which states that plants are capable of feeling emotion.
   D) None of the above are correct because there is no such thing as environmental racism.

The correct answer is A:) Any practice which harms an environment that is low income or racially homogenous more than it does other environments.

44) Which of the following BEST describes the goal of feminism?

   A) Complete political, social, and economic equality between women and men.
   B) To make it so that women can get jobs just as easily, or easier than, men.
   C) Complete political equality, which began with women suffrage in the 1920's, but continues in other ways today.
   D) Feminism has no ultimate goal.

The correct answer is A:) Complete political, social, and economic equality between women and men. Although Answers B and C both describe factors of feminism, Answer A best describes the goal.

45) Which of the following describes how Martin Luther King Jr. died?

   A) Heart attack
   B) Assassination
   C) Injuries sustained during a protest
   D) Old age

The correct answer is B:) Assassination. Martin Luther King Jr. was assassinated on April 4, 1968.

46) How does feminism apply to ethics?

   A) Feminism is just another word for ethics.
   B) The feminist movement is an attempt to ensure that there isn't unethical treatment of women.
   C) Feminism and ethics are two completely unrelated topics.
   D) The feminist movement is what caused discussions of ethics. Before that it wasn't even a word.

The correct answer is B:) The feminist movement is an attempt to ensure that there isn't unethical treatment of women. One example of a feminist success is woman suffrage.

47) Which of the following is NOT true of the story of Amos?

   A) Amos was a farmer who lived in Judah when he was called by the Lord.
   B) Judah was punished by the Lord for not repenting.
   C) The people of Israel were hardening their hearts against the Lord.
   D) Amos proclaimed the people's many sins.

The correct answer is B:) Judah was punished by the Lord for not repenting. While Amos was from Judah, he preached in Israel, and Judah wasn't involved.

48) An attorney with an obligation to manage assets to his client's best financial interest and not his own has a _____ obligation.

   A) Moral
   B) Ethical
   C) Fiduciary
   D) Integral

The correct answer is C:) Fiduciary.

49) Why is there an ethical controversy about stem cell research?

   A) Because taking cells from a person's brain stem is a dangerous process.
   B) Because taking cells from a plant's stem ruins the natural environment.
   C) Because it is a type of experimentation that almost always ends badly for the patient.
   D) Because the extraction process kills the embryo.

The correct answer is D:) Because the extraction process kills the embryo. Stem cells must be extracted from a 5-7 day old embryo, which kills it.

50) What is a patriarch?

   A) The male head of a family or tribe.
   B) A rare and beautiful bird which lives only in some South American countries.
   C) The youngest male of a Native American tribe.
   D) An extremely old book written in Egypt.

The correct answer is A:) The male head of a family or tribe.

51) What is a pacifist?

   A) A person who is morally opposed to violence and war of any kind.
   B) A group of people who protest against wars.
   C) It is the term for a company which sells pacifiers.
   D) There is no such thing as a pacifist. It is not a real term.

The correct answer is A:) A person who is morally opposed to violence and war of any kind.

52) Which of the following is NOT a central component of the ethics of care?

   A) Justice
   B) Generosity
   C) Harmony
   D) Relationships

The correct answer is A:) Justice. The ethics of justice are an opposing view to the ethics of care.

53) Which of the following is included in the UN's definition of political freedoms?

   A) Speech
   B) Media
   C) Assembly
   D) All of the above

The correct answer is D:) All of the above. Also included are the freedoms of expression, information, association and suffrage.

54) Who is noted for developing the principle of double effect?

   A) Thomas Aquinas
   B) Ayn Rand
   C) Ronald Dworkin
   D) Friedrich Nietzsche

The correct answer is A:) Thomas Aquinas. Aquinas developed four standards by which an action could be justifiable despite negative consequences. This is referred to as the principle of double effect.

55) Tenements were

   A) Laws passed in the south after the Civil War which promoted segregation and racism.
   B) Upscale neighborhoods which developed in highly urban cities.
   C) Regulations which attempted to control the development of monopolies.
   D) Poorly constructed and overcrowded housing for poor urban workers.

The correct answer is D:) Poorly constructed and overcrowded housing for poor urban workers. Rapid urbanization caused a lack of good public health programs and a shortage of housing.

56) Which of the following moral theories is NOT consequentialist?

   A) Teleology
   B) Act utilitarianism
   C) Egoism
   D) Kantian ethics

The correct answer is D:) Kantian ethics. Kantian ethics determines morality based on the morality of the action itself, not its consequences. It is deontological.

57) Which of the following best describes rule utilitarianism?

   A) A person considers an action independently of a situation and determines whether it is more often moral or immoral to determine how to classify it in all situations.
   B) A person considers a situation and decides upon the easiest course of action.
   C) A person considers an action and determines whether it would end favorably for them.
   D) A person examines a situation, considers all possible actions they could take and decides which one would end most favorably for all involved.

The correct answer is A:) A person considers an action independently of a situation and determines whether it is more often moral or immoral to determine how to classify it in all situations.

58) A person is given the opportunity to volunteer at a local food bank. They consider the other things they could do at that time, such as cleaning and watching TV. They know that the work that they do could really benefit people at the food bank, whereas the other activities only benefit themselves. They decide that the service is the best decision for them. What type of ethical theory does their thought process and decision follow?

   A) Rule utilitarianism
   B) Act utilitarianism
   C) Deontological theory
   D) Ethical egoism

The correct answer is B:) Act utilitarianism. A person examines a situation, considers all possible actions they could take and decides which one would end most favorably for all involved.

59) Which of the following terms is most synonymous with philanthropy?

   A) Implied falsity
   B) Reciprocity
   C) Altruism
   D) Egoism

The correct answer is C:) Altruism. Altruism refers to placing the needs of another above oneself, such as through philanthropic acts. Reciprocity is the idea of treating others how you would wish to be treated.

60) Cost benefit considerations would be most typical of which of type of ethics?

A) Consequentialism
B) Egoism
C) Kantian
D) Utilitarianism

The correct answer is D:) Utilitarianism. The idea behind utilitarianism is to "maximize utility." In other words the focus is on considering the benefits and costs and if the benefits are greater than the costs then the action is moral.

61) Which of the following terms describes a moral theory which derives morality from actions?

A) Teleological ethics
B) Consequentialism
C) Deontological ethics
D) None of the above

The correct answer is C:) Deontological ethics. Deontological ethics claims that the morality of an action is determined by the morality of the action itself – regardless of the consequence.

62) What is environmental justice?

A) When companies consider environmental issues when they make business decisions.
B) When issues are brought before a court which involve environmental factors.
C) A move toward equality among all races in issues relating to environmental hazards.
D) A collective movement by governments worldwide to decrease the emission of greenhouse gases.

The correct answer is C:) A move toward equality among all races in issues relating to environmental hazards.

63) Which of the following is the BEST example of a metaethical question?

   A) Is it wrong to murder someone?
   B) How is morality defined?
   C) Is stealing moral?
   D) Should I lie to protect my family?

The correct answer is B:) How is morality defined? Metaethics is the branch of ethics that seeks to understand and define the underlying principles of ethics so that they can be more accurately applied.

64) Which of the following is NOT a criteria that supports an action under the principle of double effects?

   A) The primary motivation must be the good consequences of the action
   B) An action must be inherently good or inherently neutral
   C) The negative effect must be equal to or greater than the positive effect
   D) A bad action cannot be used to justify a good consequence

The correct answer is C:) The negative effect must be equal to or greater than the positive effect. The opposite is true. According to the principle of double effects an action is only justifiable moral if the good effects it produces are in proportion to the negative effects.

65) Objectivism is the theory developed by

   A) Thomas Aquinas
   B) Jane English
   C) Friedrich Nietzsche
   D) Ayn Rand

The correct answer is D:) Ayn Rand. Rand argues that principles of reality, reason, and free will are what determine the morality of an action.

66) Which of the following statements BEST characterizes the theories of Friedrich Nietzsche?

   A) Human decisions are made egoistically. Individuals are incapable of acting in any other way.
   B) Truth exists, and it is unchanging and fixed. Reason must be used to determine truth.
   C) Decisions, morality, and religion ultimately have no effect and are meaningless.
   D) The best decisions in life are those which minimize the collective negative consequences.

The correct answer is C:) Decisions, morality, and religion ultimately have no effect and are meaningless. Nietzsche was known for his work in popularizing the theory of Nihilism. This theory rejects notions of morality and essentially claims that all things are meaningless.

67) Which of the following BEST describes the beliefs of philosophy Joel Feinberg?

   A) Human decisions are made egoistically. Individuals are incapable of acting in any other way.
   B) Truth exists, and it is unchanging and fixed. Reason must be used to determine truth.
   C) Decisions, morality, and religion ultimately have no effect and are meaningless.
   D) The best decisions in life are those which minimize the collective negative consequences.

The correct answer is A:) Human decisions are made egoistically. Individuals are incapable of acting in any other way. Joel Feinberg was well known for his support of the ethical theories of psychological egoism. Psychological egoism is a theory which argues that people always act according to their own best interests.

68) Legal interpretivism was a theory developed by

   A) David Gauthier
   B) Jane English
   C) Ronald Dworkin
   D) Joel Feinberg

The correct answer is C:) Ronald Dworkin. Dworkin was born in 1931 in Rhode Island, and went on to amaze professors at both Harvard and Oxford. Legal interpretivism rejected the traditions views of the objectivity of law, and instead claimed that they law was open to interpretation.

69) Which of the following best describes the beliefs of philosopher David Gauthier?

A) Human decisions are made egoistically. Individuals are incapable of acting in any other way.
B) Truth exists, and it is unchanging and fixed. Reason must be used to determine truth.
C) Decisions, morality, and religion ultimately have no effect and are meaningless.
D) The best decisions in life are those which minimize the collective negative consequences.

The correct answer is D:) The best decisions in life are those which minimize the collective negative consequences. This is known as the theory of morals by agreement. Gauthier argued that the greatest benefit to mankind comes when individual cooperate, and that requires personal sacrifice.

70) The theories of Jane English particularly center around

A) Fidelity
B) Legal interpretations
C) Abortion
D) Justifiability of war

The correct answer is C:) Abortion. Jane English is a philosopher well known for her feminist and gender related theories. In terms of abortion, English argues that there is no single factor that justifies or eliminates the morality of abortion.

71) Which of the following ethical terms is synonymous with honesty?

A) Autonomy
B) Fidelity
C) Veracity
D) Duty

The correct answer is C:) Veracity. Veracity refers to honesty and truthfulness. A veracious person is a person who is always truthful.

72) Which of the following is NOT a justification for war under the just war theory?

   A) Just objective
   B) Just authority
   C) Just cause
   D) Just intention

The correct answer is A:) Just objective. The just war theory states that there are four qualifications that, if met, make the act of war morally justifiable.

73) Which principle is used to describe the obligations an individual is expected to fulfill?

   A) Fidelity
   B) Veracity
   C) Justice
   D) Duty

The correct answer is D:) Duty. Duty refers to moral or legal obligations that an individual is expect to fulfill. It is a key aspect of many ethical theories.

74) In which case did the Supreme Court establish that segregation in public schools was unconstitutional?

   A) Brown v. Board of Education
   B) Roe v. Wade
   C) Plessy v. Ferguson
   D) MuCulloch v. Maryland

The correct answer is A:) Brown v. Board of Education. This overturned the case of Plessy v. Ferguson which allowed "separate but equal" schools.

75) Which of the following statements INCORRECTLY describes Kant's theory?

   A) He believed that for a principle to be correct it had to be universal.
   B) Kant's theories directly opposed the theories of the Enlightenment.
   C) He believed that universality would make ethical principles irrefutable.
   D) Kant argued that since reason could explain physical laws, it could explain moral laws as well.

The correct answer is B:) Kant's theories directly opposed the theories of the Enlightenment. Kant was actually one of the supporters of the Enlightenment. He supported reason and rationality as the basis for ethical principles.

76) A doctor educates their patient about all of the possible treatments that they could take before allowing them to choose the one that they feel best. This is an example of promoting which ethical principle?

A) Duty
B) Justification
C) Decisiveness
D) Autonomy

The correct answer is D:) Autonomy. Autonomy is a principle of self-choice. However, in order for autonomy to be properly exercised, an individual must have awareness of the facts and be prepared to act in their own best interest as well.

77) Which of the following would be considered an example of speciesism?

A) In some countries it is illegal to eat certain types of meat
B) Countries ruled by a dictator are more likely to go to war
C) A doctor is expected to give all patients equal treatment
D) The punishment for killing a human is more severe than the punishment for killing a fish

The correct answer is D:) The punishment for killing a human is more severe than the punishment for killing a fish. Speciesism is discrimination based on species. It can refer to humans being given legal precedence over other species, or to other nonhuman species that are treated unequally.

78) By passing laws, governments effectively dictate many of the decisions individuals can and cannot make. Some consider this to be an example of

A) Paternalism
B) Euthanasia
C) Fidelity
D) State of nature

The correct answer is A:) Paternalism. Paternalism refers to any situation in which one party in a position of authority exercises control over another.

79) Utilitarianism requires that individuals seek to maximize the general good. This requires a process of

   A) Metaethics
   B) Speciesism
   C) Paternalism
   D) Balancing harms

The correct answer is D:) Balancing harms. To determine which actions allow for the greatest good to society, it is often necessary to consider the harms that come to some individuals. Because resources are finite, benefits to one individual necessarily restrict benefits to another.

80) Which of the following terms is used to describe actions taken to prevent harm to others?

   A) Informed consent
   B) Non-malfeasance
   C) Beneficence
   D) Euthanasia

The correct answer is B:) Non-malfeasance. Whereas beneficence refers to actions taken to benefit others, non-malfeasance is the ethical obligation to prevent harm to others.

81) According to Aristotle, a vice is

   A) A virtue that is not fully exercised
   B) A virtue that is exercised too intensely
   C) A virtue that is rarely found in society
   D) Both A and B

The correct answer is D:) Both A and B. Aristotle was known for his study of virtues and vices. He argued that any virtue could become a vice if taken too far, or if not fully developed. For example, courage, if taken too far, could lead an individual to be overly rash. On the other hand, if not fully developed, courage gives way to cowardice.

82) According to traditional philosophy, a state of nature is essentially the equivalent of

   A) Anarchy
   B) Utilitarianism
   C) Utopia
   D) Veracity

The correct answer is A:) Anarchy. A state of nature denotes the natural state of society without the existence of government. Most traditional philosophy views this as a state of anarchy and confusion.

83) A doctor recommends a treatment option without explaining the possible negative consequences of it. This violates which ethical principle?

   A) State of nature
   B) Informed consent
   C) Malfeasance
   D) Fidelity

The correct answer is B:) Informed consent. The principle of informed consent requires that an individual is aware of all of their options and the possible consequences of them. This allows an individual to fully exercise their free will in making a decision.

84) An individual believes that stealing is immoral because it is against the Ten Commandments given by God in the Old Testament. This is an example of

   A) Paternalism
   B) Theological moralism
   C) Divine command theory
   D) Balancing harms theory

The correct answer is C:) Divine command theory. This is a moral theory arguing that morality is determined by the commands of God. Any action commanded by God is moral.

85) Which of the following ethical terms is synonymous with loyalty?

   A) Autonomy
   B) Fidelity
   C) Veracity
   D) Duty

The correct answer is B:) Fidelity. Fidelity refers to loyalty and faithfulness in one's dealings with another person. It is an important principle of ethics that a person is genuine and loyal.

86) What was Amos's message?

   A) Israel will not be punished by the Lord for their sins because they are his chosen people.
   B) Judah will be punished because they are not righteous.
   C) All people are on the same level in God's eyes.
   D) Israel is higher in God's eyes because they are his chosen people.

The correct answer is C:) All people are on the same level in God's eyes. They are all expected to be righteous and pure no matter what their circumstances are.

Test-Taking Strategies

Here are some test-taking strategies that are specific to this test and to other DSST tests in general:

- Keep your eyes on the time. Pay attention to how much time you have left.

- Read the entire question and read all the answers. Many questions are not as hard to answer as they may seem. Sometimes, a difficult sounding question really only is asking you how to read an accompanying chart. Chart and graph questions are on most DANTES/DSST tests and should be an easy free point.

- If you don't know the answer immediately, the new computer-based testing lets you mark questions and come back to them later if you have time.

- Read the wording carefully. Some words can give you hints to the right answer. There are no exceptions to an answer when there are words in the question such as always, all or none. If one of the answer choices includes most or some of the right answers, but not all, then that is not the answer. Here is an example:

The primary colors include all of the following:

A) Red, Yellow, Blue, Green

B) Red, Green, Yellow

C) Red, Orange, Yellow

D) Red, Yellow, Blue

Although item A includes all the right answers, it also includes an incorrect answer, making it incorrect. If you didn't read it carefully, were in a hurry, or didn't know the material well, you might fall for this.

- Make a guess on a question that you do not know the answer to. There is no penalty for an incorrect answer. Eliminate the answer choices that you know are incorrect. For example, this will let your guess be a 1 in 3 chance instead.

Test Preparation

How much you need to study depends on your knowledge of a subject area. If you are interested in literature, took it in school, or enjoy reading then your study and preparation for the literature or humanities test will not need to be as intensive as that of someone who is new to literature.

This book is much different than the regular DANTES study guides. This book actually teaches you the information that you need to know to pass the test. If you are particularly interested in an area, or feel that you want more information, do a quick search online. We've tried not to include too much depth in areas that are not as essential on the test. Everything in this book will be on the test. It is important to understand all major theories and concepts listed in the table of contents. It is also important to know any bolded words.

Don't worry if you do not understand or know a lot about the area. With minimal study, you can complete and pass the test.

Legal Note

All rights reserved. This Study Guide, Book and Flashcards are protected under US Copyright Law. No part of this book or study guide or flashcards may be reproduced, distributed or stored in a retrieval system, or transmitted in any form or by any means, electronic, mechanical, photocopying, recording, or otherwise, without the prior written permission of the publisher Breely Crush Publishing, LLC. This manual is not supported by or affiliated with the College Board, creators of the CLEP test or Prometric, creators of the DSST test. CLEP is a registered trademark of the College Entrance Examination Board, which does not endorse this book. DSST is a registered trademark of Prometric which does not endorse this book.

FLASHCARDS

This section contains flashcards for you to use to further your understanding of the material and test yourself on important concepts, names or dates. Read the term or question then flip the page over to check the answer on the back. Keep in mind that this information may not be covered in the text of the study guide. Take your time to study the flashcards, you will need to know and understand these concepts to pass the test.

Allegory of the Cave

Ahimsa

Sermon on the Mount

"Nicomachean Ethics" was written by

Socratic Method

Law of Retaliation

Plato wrote a book entitled "Plato's _____"

"The Peloponnesian" War was written by

Do no harm	Famous passage of Plato's Republic
Aristotle	A summary of Christian ethical beliefs
An eye for an eye	A way of argument in which a person seeks to discover the truth about a certain issue
Thucydides	Republic

"The Enneads" was written by	Native Americans view the land
First Principle	Amos
Equity	Plotinus believed in what forms?
Allegory of the Cave	Active euthanasia

As more of a consciousness	Plotinus
Proclaimed that all people are on the same level in God's eyes	A way as to help a person's Soul transcend all Being and bring happiness
Beauty, Largeness, Smallness	The solution to any disparity between natural justice and legal justice
When a person actually does something to end a patient's life	Socrates

Eudaimonia	Aristotle felt that having ____ was a key component to a happy life
Natural law	St. Thomas Aquinas
Hobbes, Locke and Rousseau	Tuskegee Syphilis Experiment
Henry David Thoreau	Who wrote "The Sand County Almanac"?

Voluntary action	Ongoing sense of happiness in your life
A moral theory that was focused around the idea of natural law	The moral standards that determine our human behavior
Pertains to informed consent	Political theorists
Aldo Leopold	Civil Disobedience

"I heartily accept the motto, "That government is best which governs least"	"The tree of liberty must be refreshed from time to time with the blood of patriots and tyrants."
"I have a dream…"	Belmont Report
"I believe in equality for everyone, except reporters and photographers!"	One of the greatest values people have
Secondary virtue	"Man was born free, and everywhere he is in chains."

Thomas Jefferson	Henry David Thoreau
set forth guidelines for human experimentation	Dr. Martin Luther King
Freedom	Mahatma Gandhi
Jacques Rousseau	Loyalty

John Rawls	"Justice as Fairness" theory
Hedonism	Who believed in "might makes right"?
Jeremy Bentham	"Principle of utility" or "greatest happiness principle"
Felicific Calculus	"No society is truly free unless its individual citizens are permitted to take care of themselves."

"The liberty principle" and "the difference principle"	A Theory of Justice
Thrasymachus	The belief that happiness is obtained through the pleasures of the senses
Pleasure and pain were the only true absolutes in the entire world	"Principle of utility" or "greatest happiness principle"
John Stuart Mill	Method for calculating the total amount of pleasure and pain that comes from an action

Rita Manning	Carol Gilligan

Peripatetic School	Pacifist

Socrates was accused of what crime?	Example of special moral relationship

Griswold vs. Connecticut	Veracity

Thought that women followed a different course than men in their moral development	Ethics of Care
Opposed to violence and war of any kind	Aristotle
Parent - child	Corrupting youth
Being truthful	Right to privacy

Affirmative action	ISO
Three first professions	Paternalism
Retributive justice	Distributive justice
Balancing harms	"All the Law and the Prophets hang upon the Two Great Commandments, to love thy Lord God and to love thy neighbor."

International Organization for Standardization	Benefiting underrepresented groups by taking factors such as race, gender, or religion into account in business and educational settings
The way people are governed or treated by an authority	Medicine, law and the ministry
With a strict or radical form of equality that is said to be necessary for all people	Theory that punishments are justified because criminals create an imbalance in the order of society which has to be taken care of by action
Jesus Christ, New Testament	Balancing the harms that exist in both sides of the example of an ethical situation

Paradox	Prohairesis
Dihairesis	Mary Wollstonecraft
Lawrence Kohlberg	Environmental racism
Goal of feminism	What are stem cells?

Called the distinguishing factor that separated human beings from all other creatures on the planet	Something that seems to be contradictory and yet may nonetheless be true
Feminist philosopher and writer	The judgement itself that was made by a person's Prohairesis
Any practice which harms an environment that is low income, or where a specific race (often minority) is prevalent, more than it does other environments	Moral development was a six-stage process
Cells which have the potential to become any type of cell	Complete equality between women and men